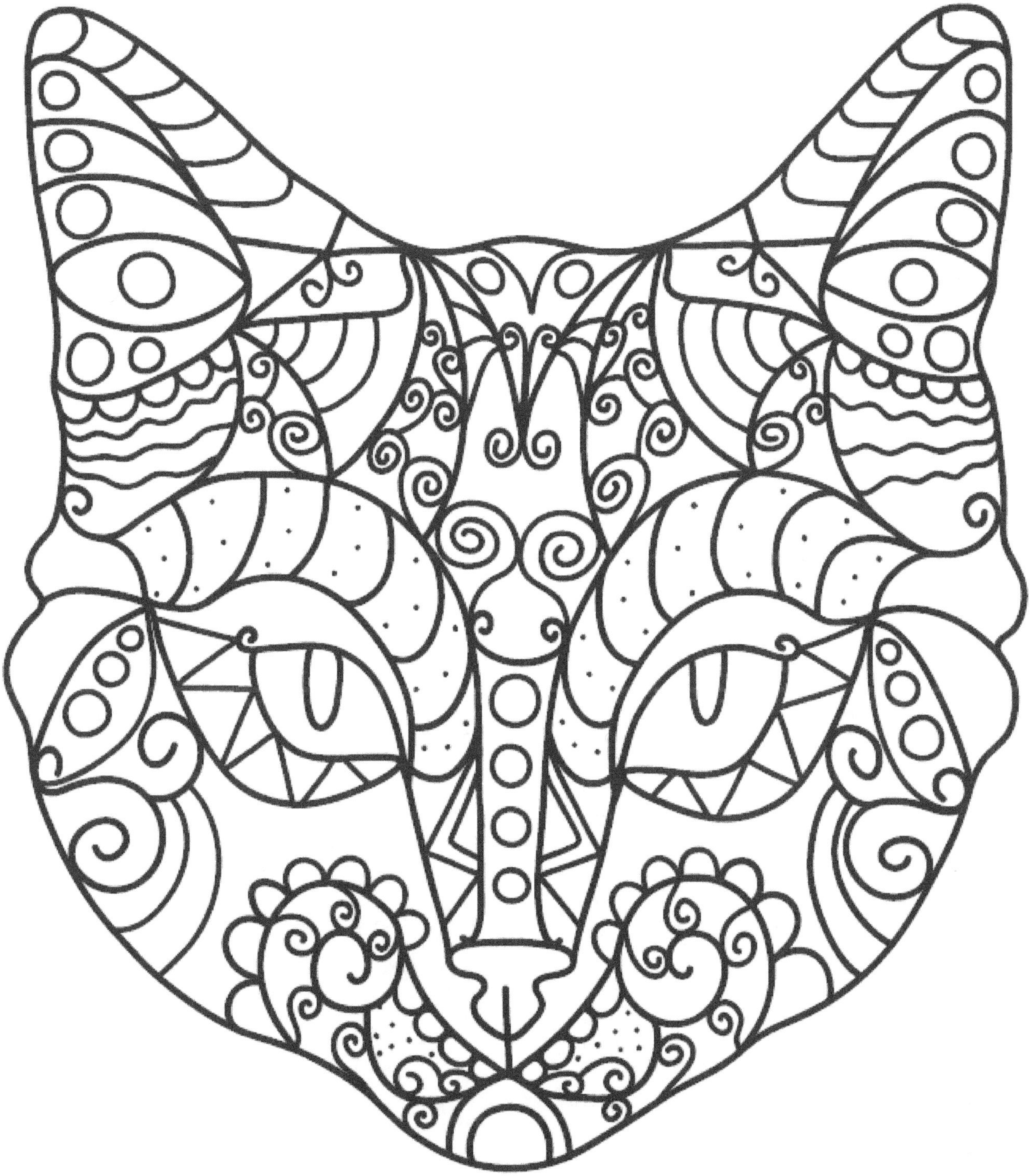

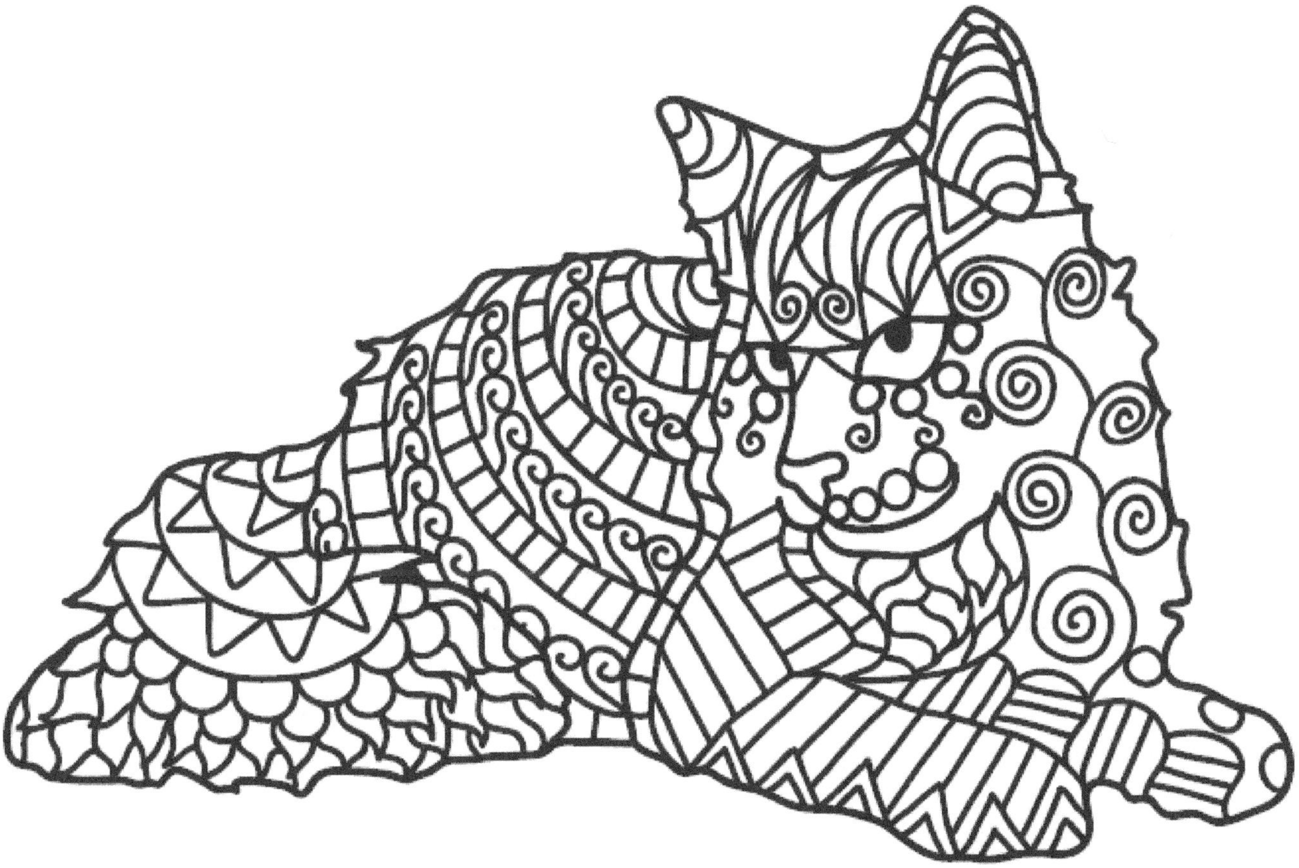

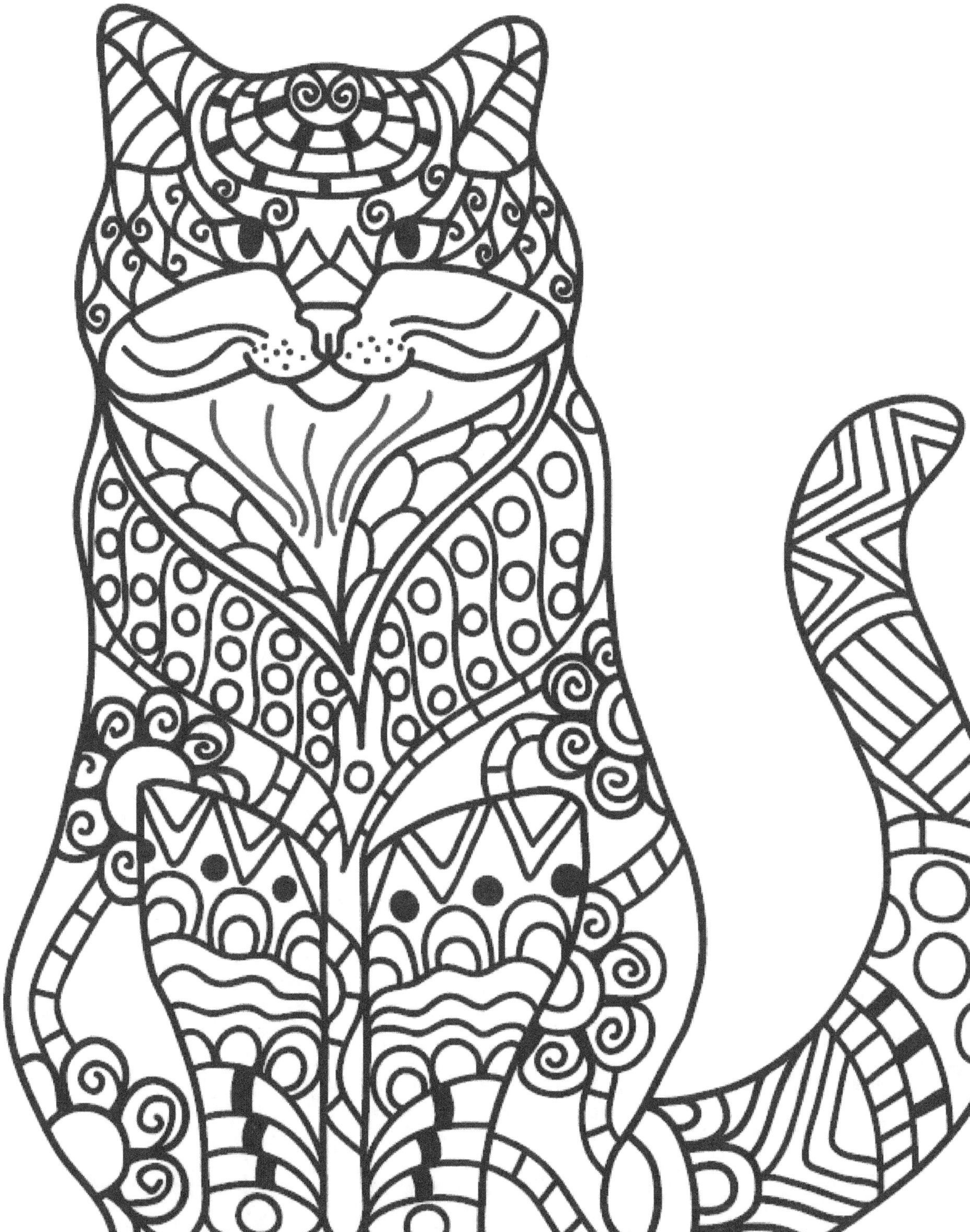

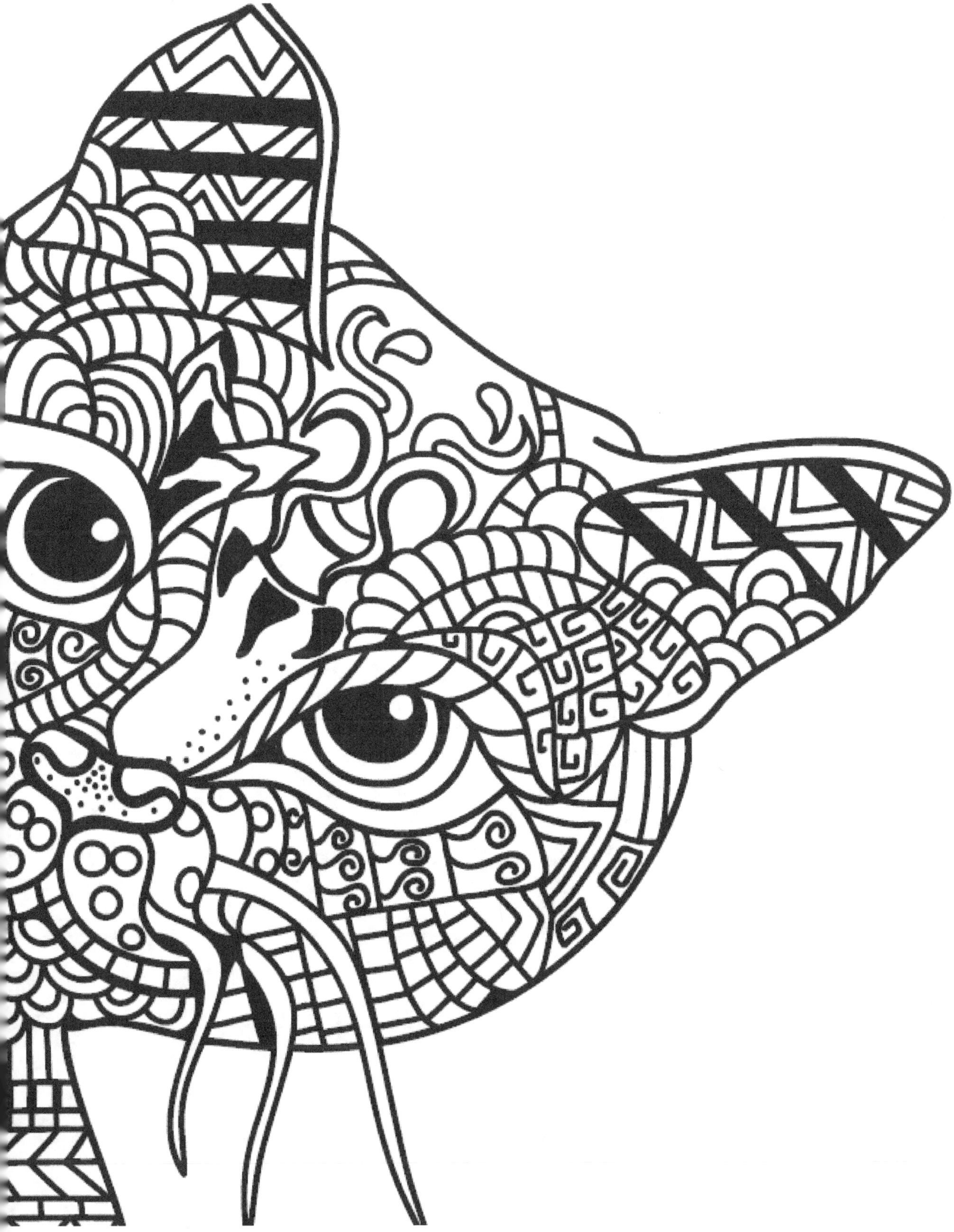

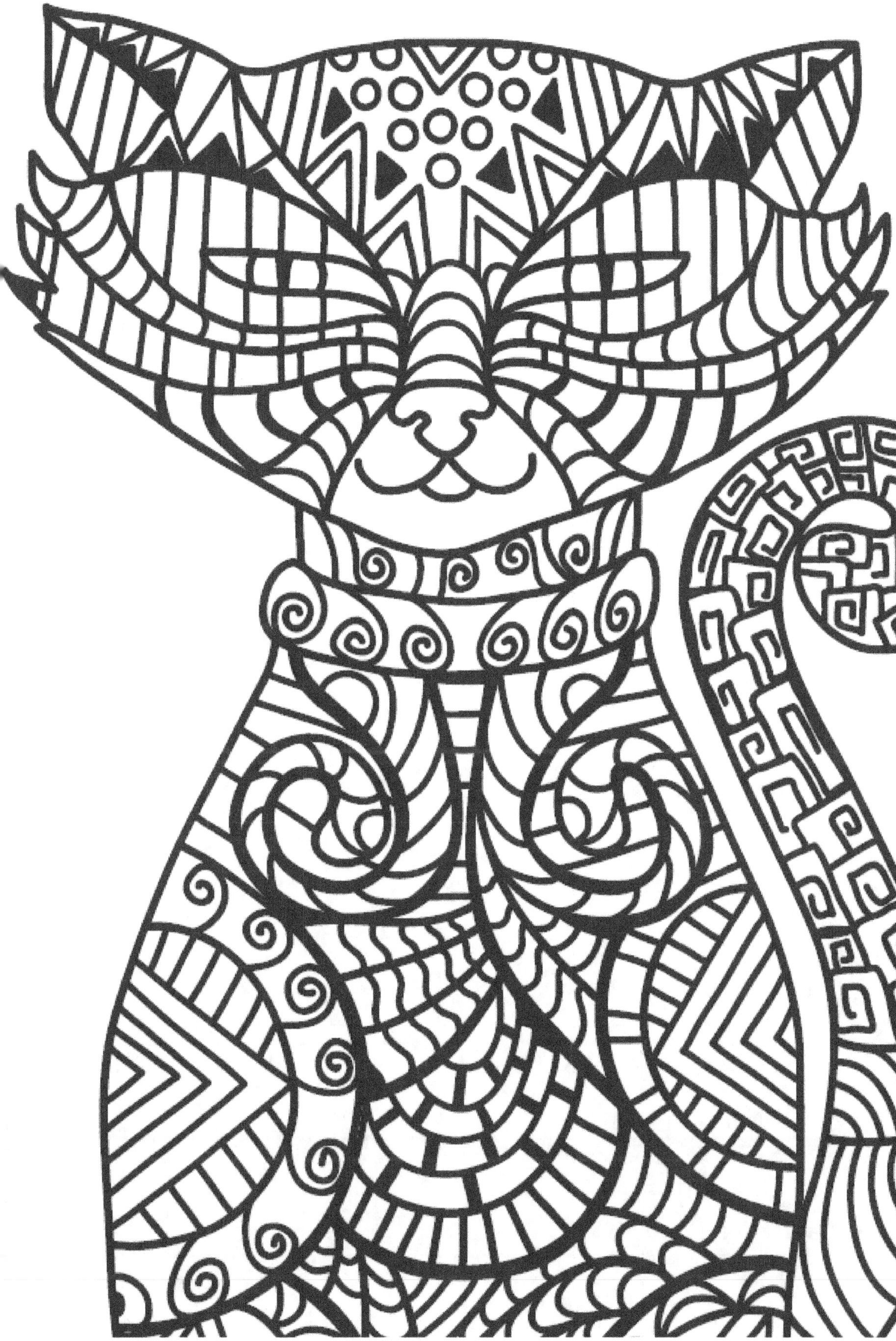

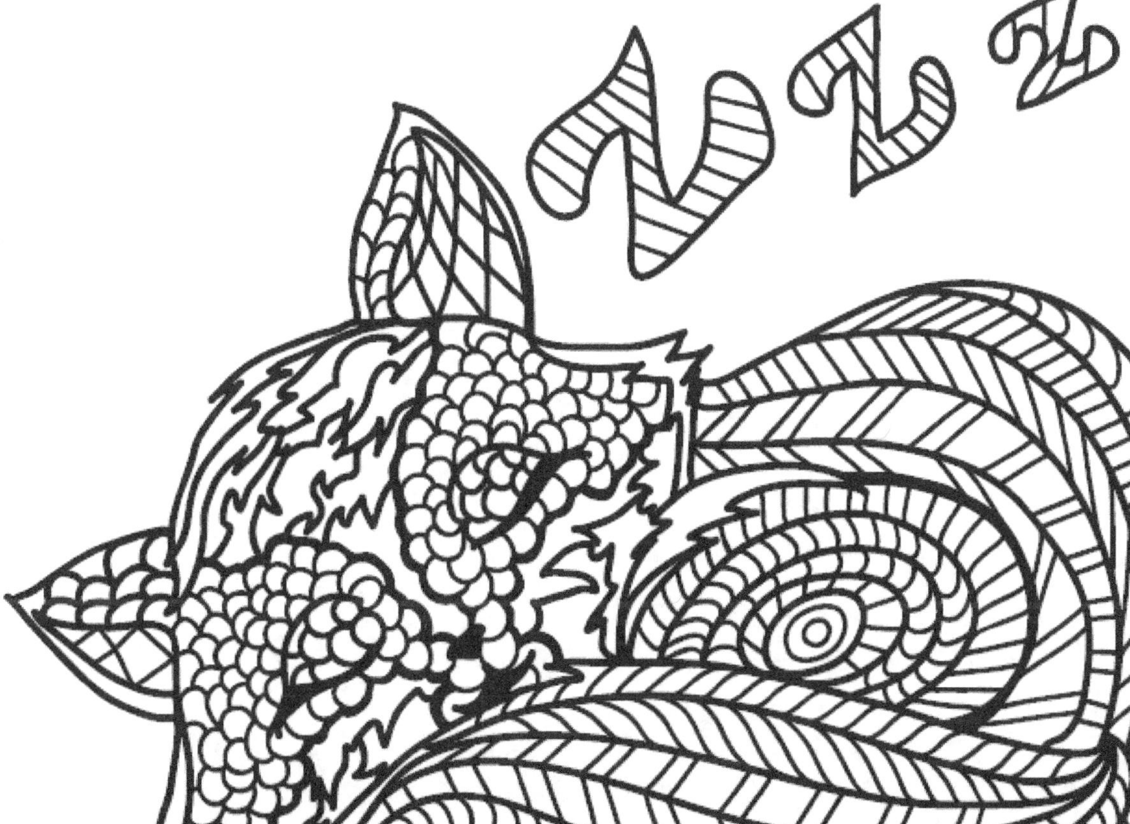
Z Z z

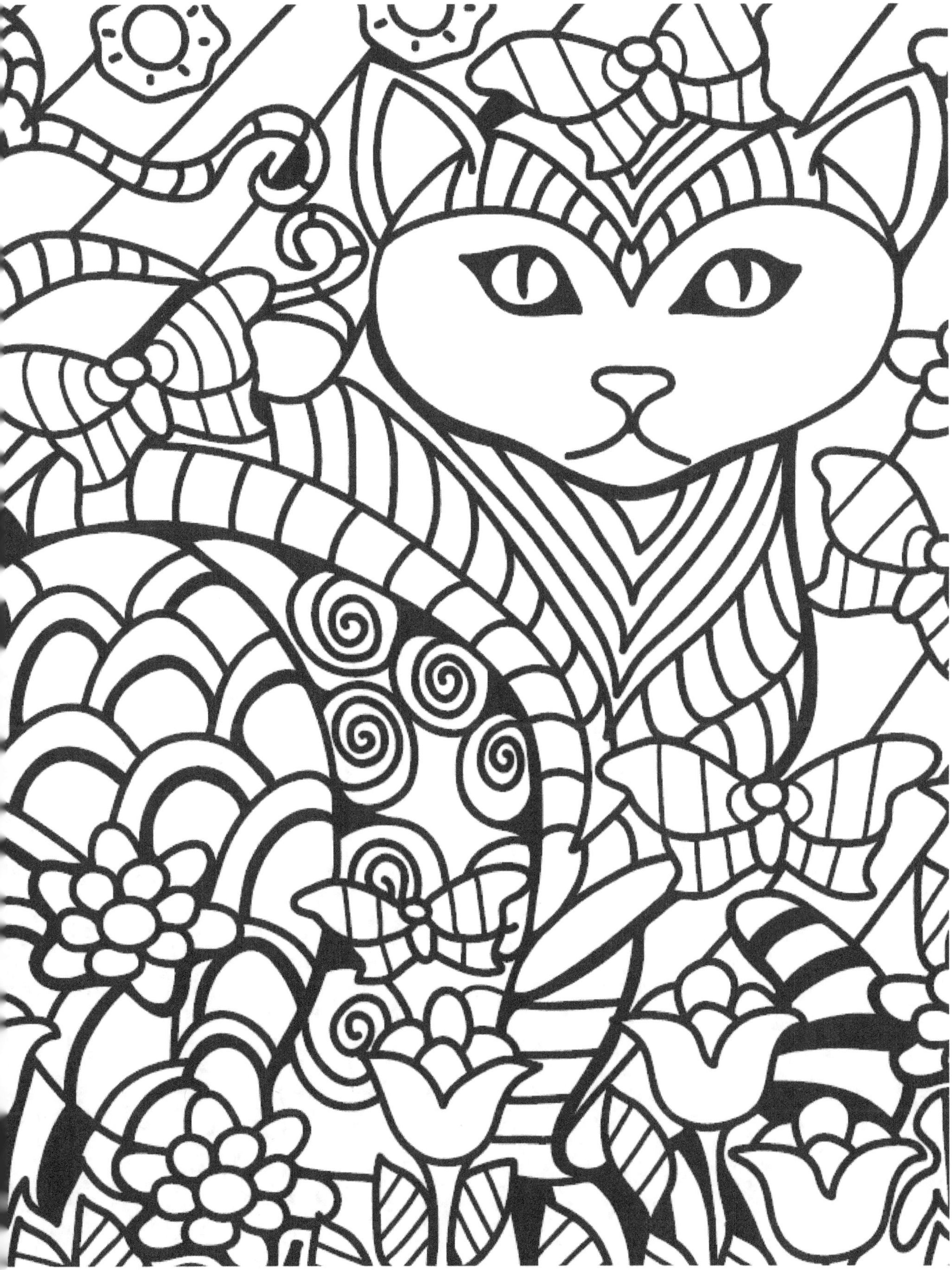

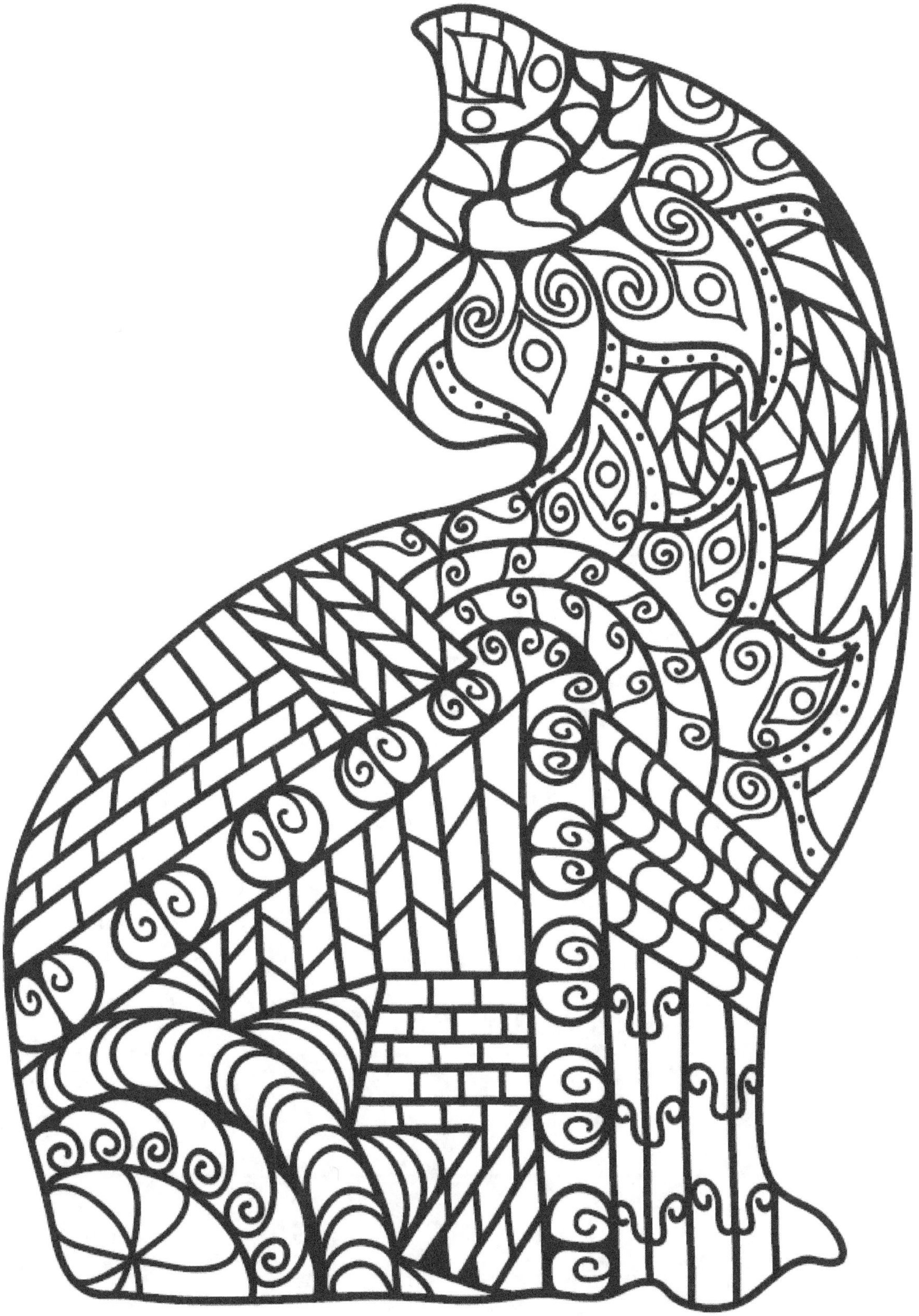

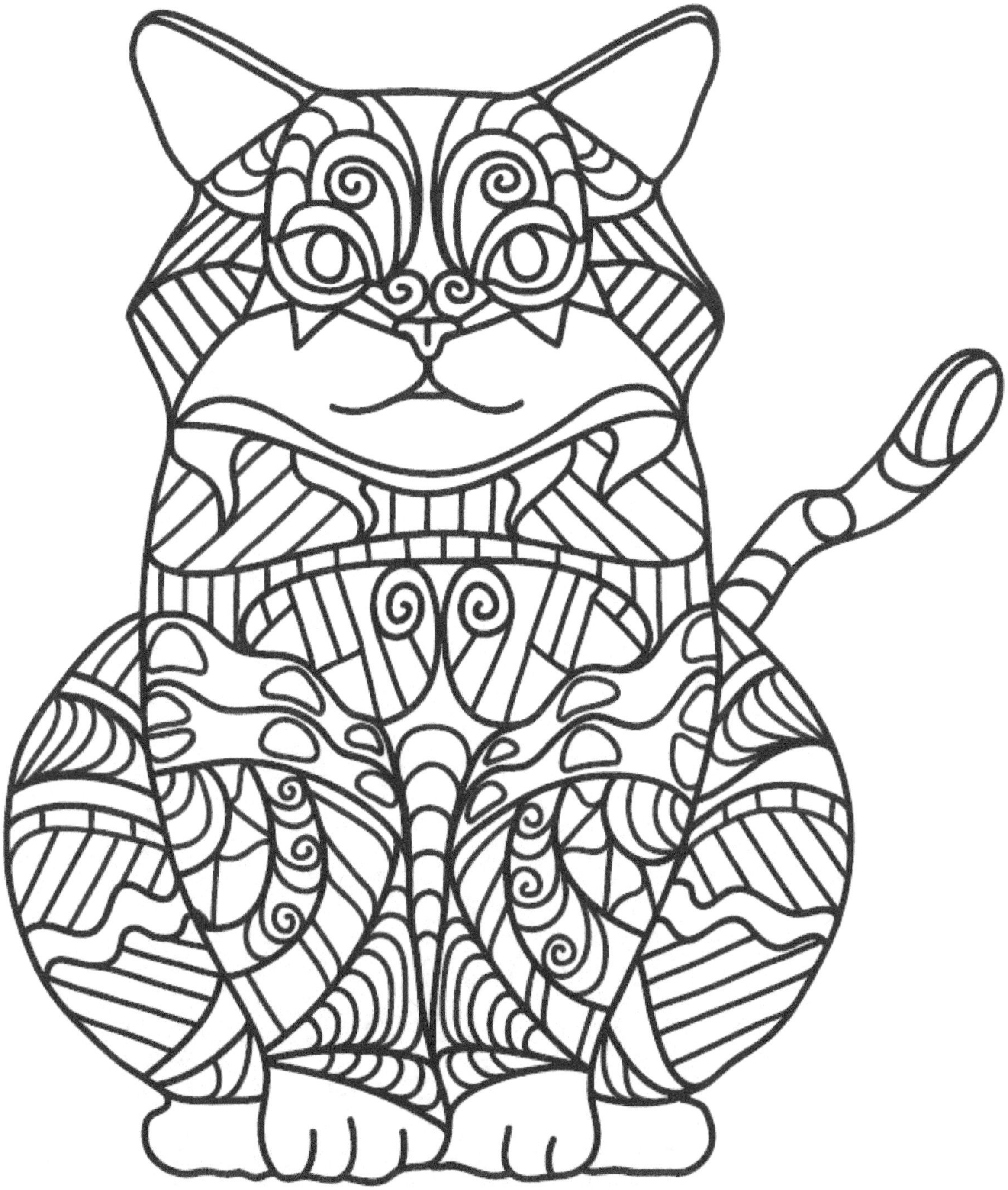

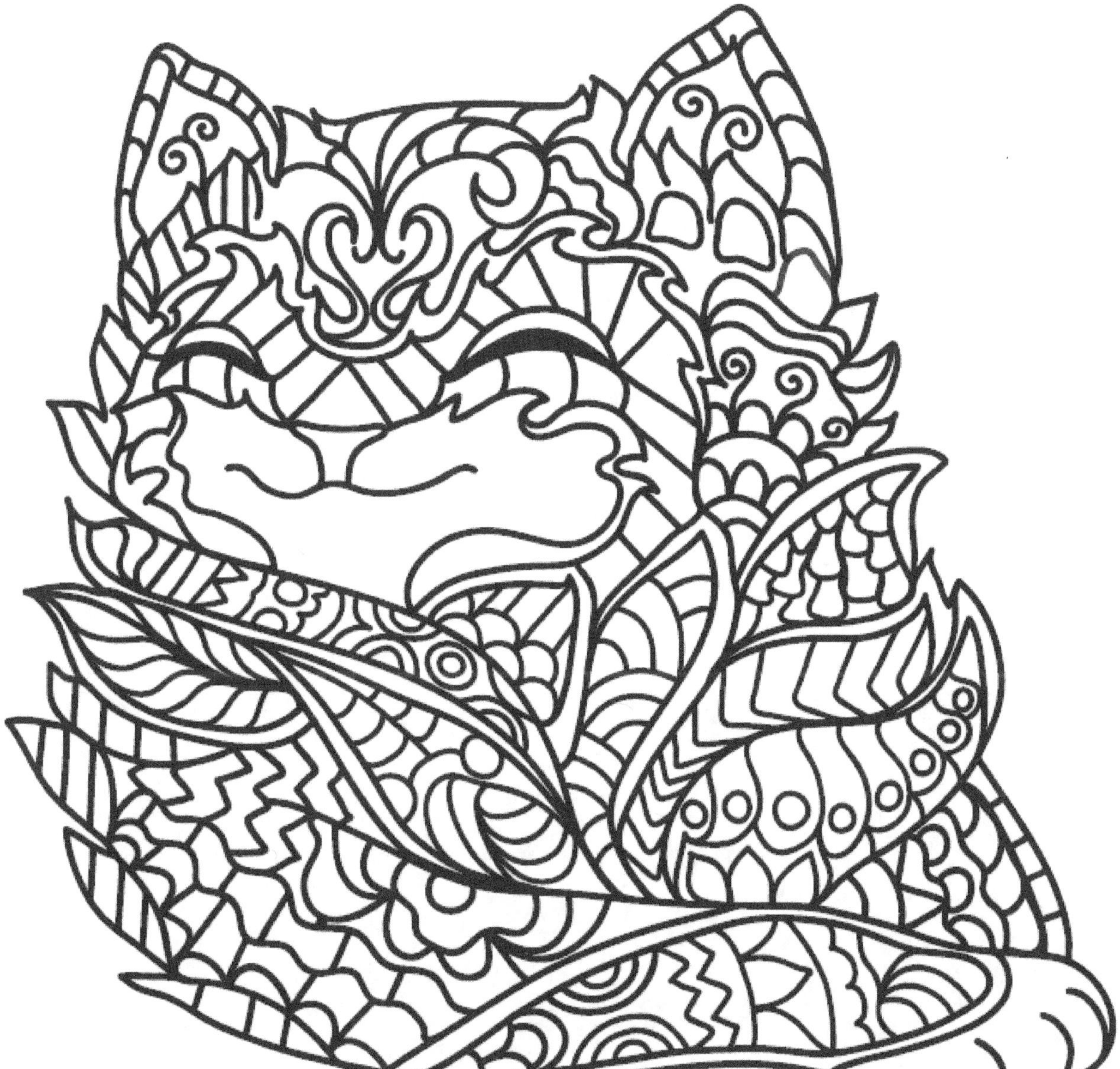

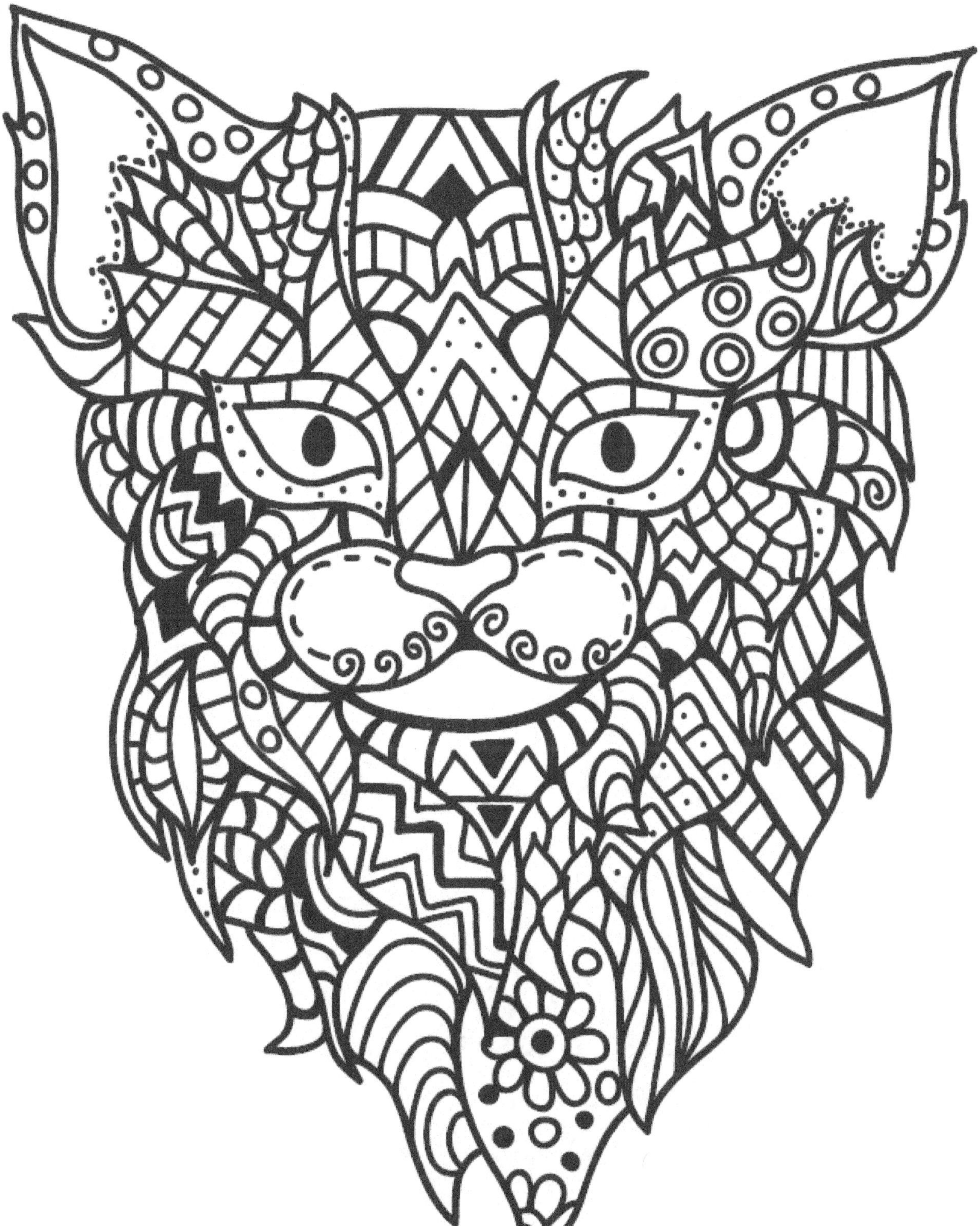

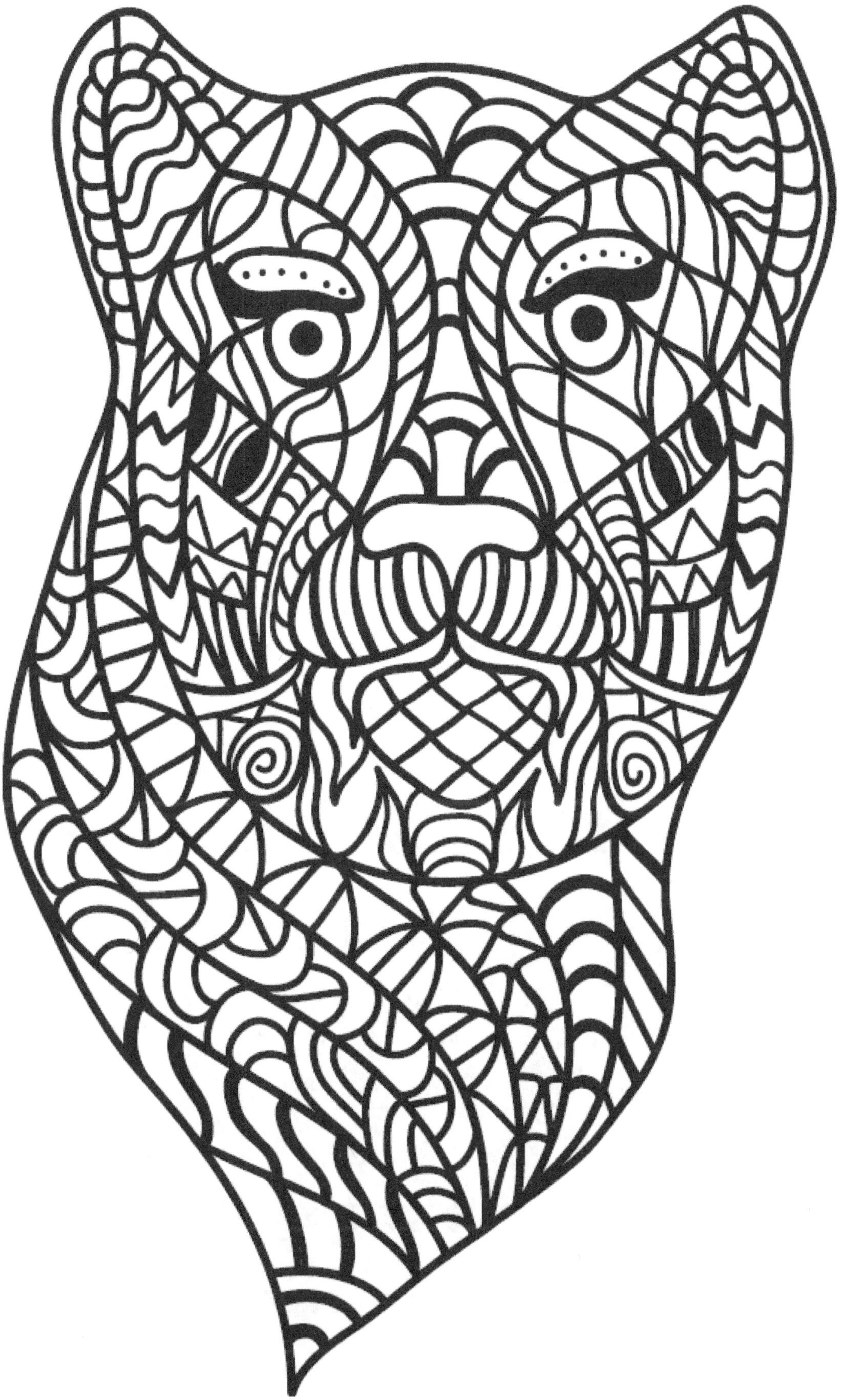

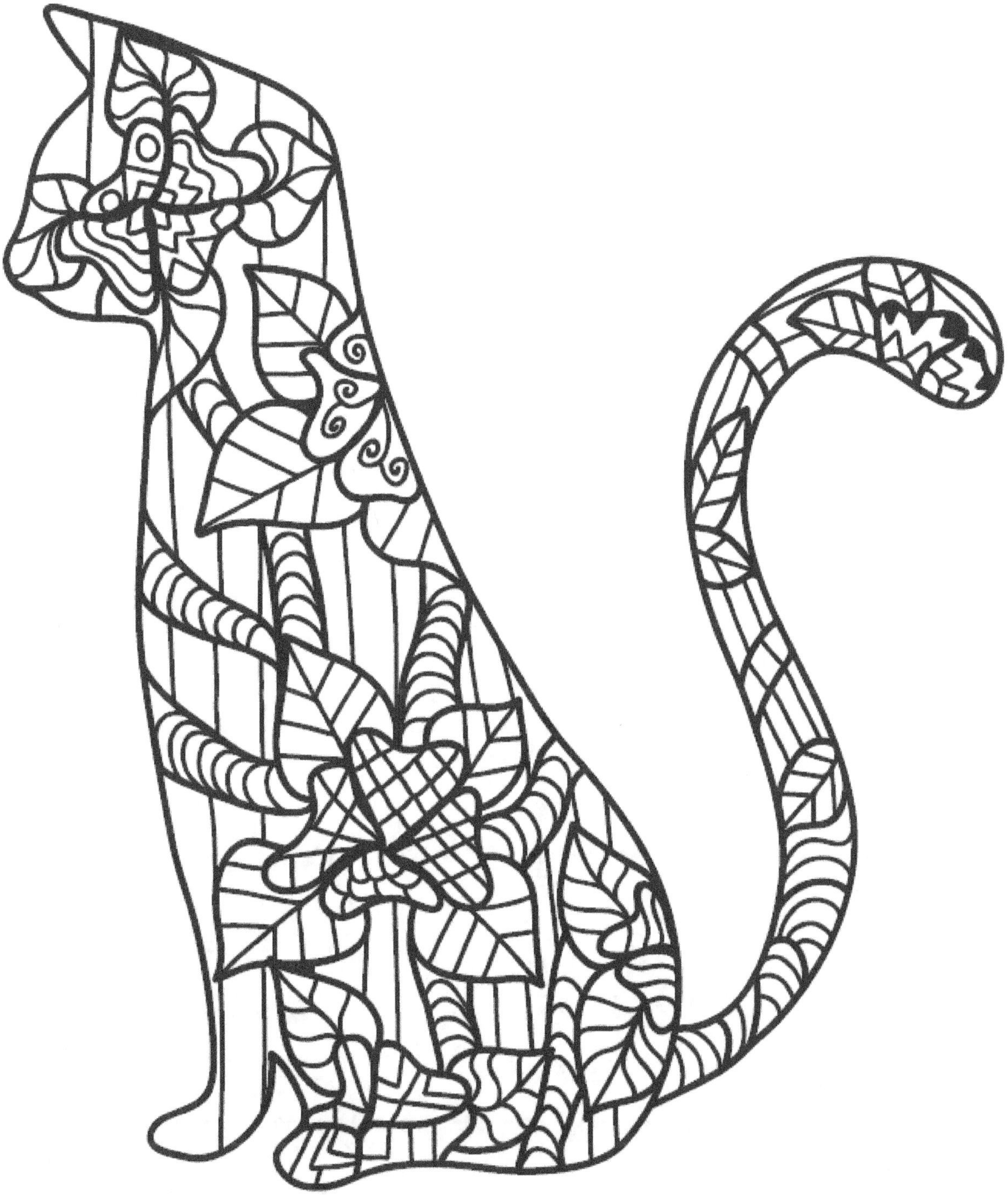

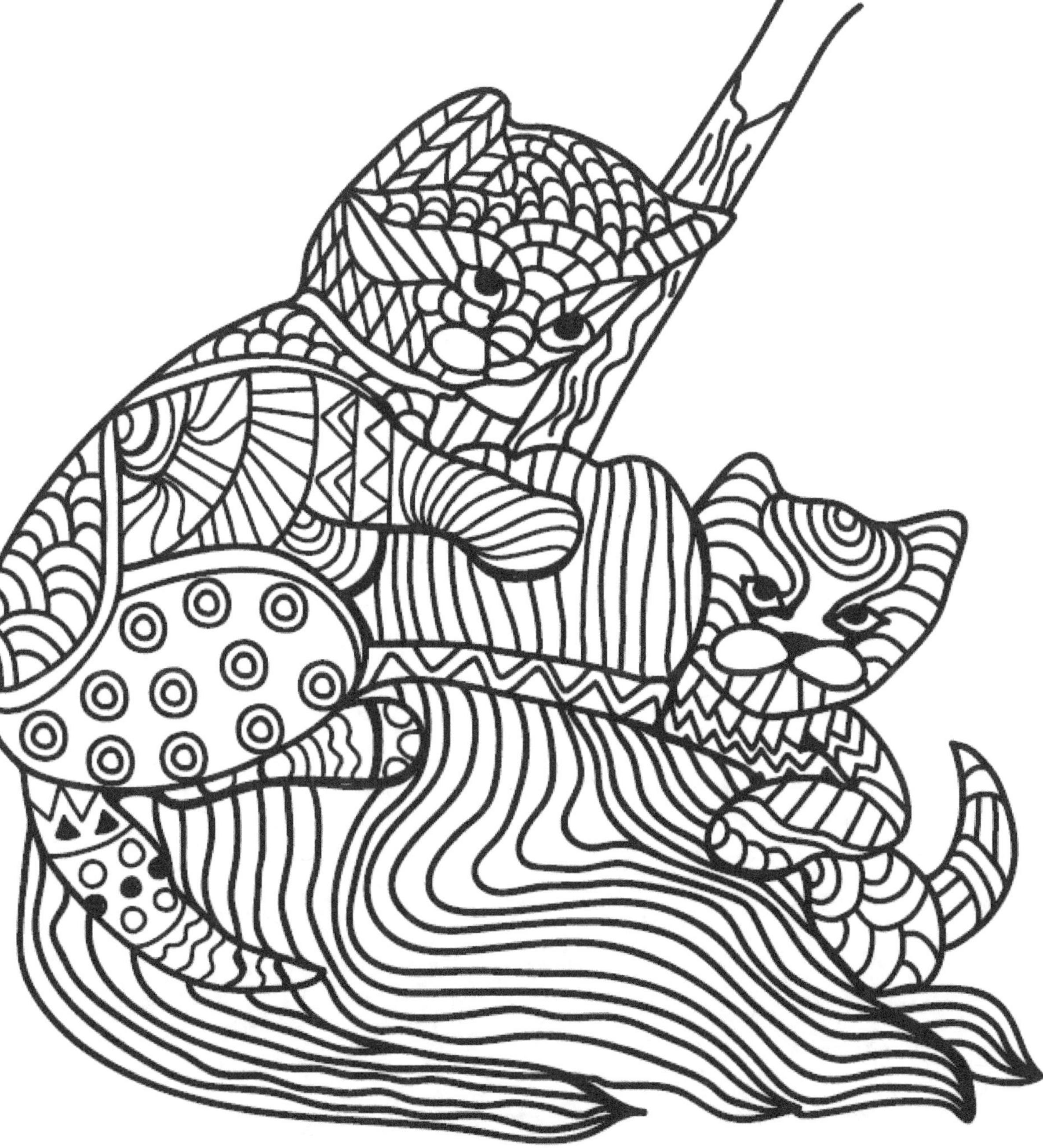

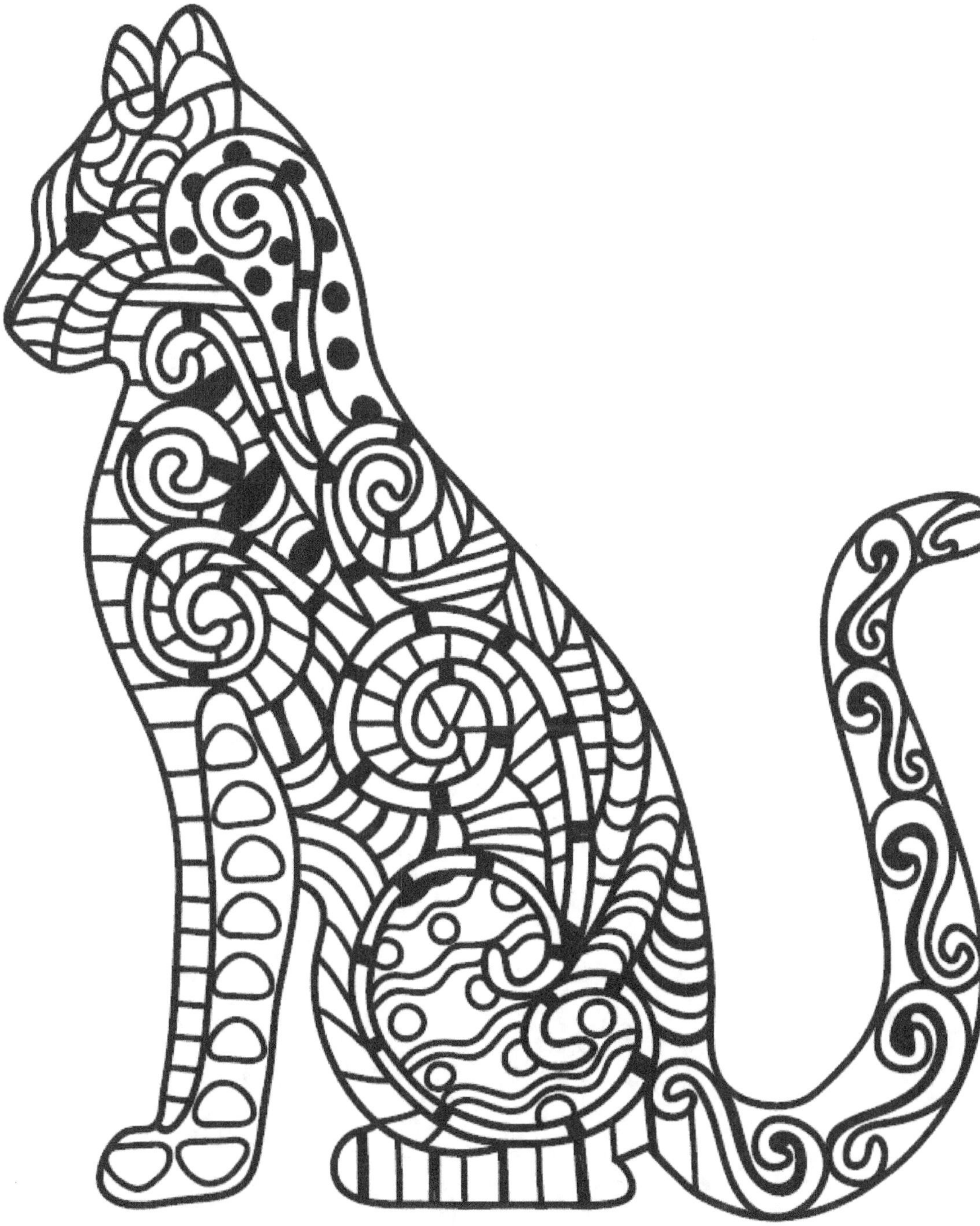

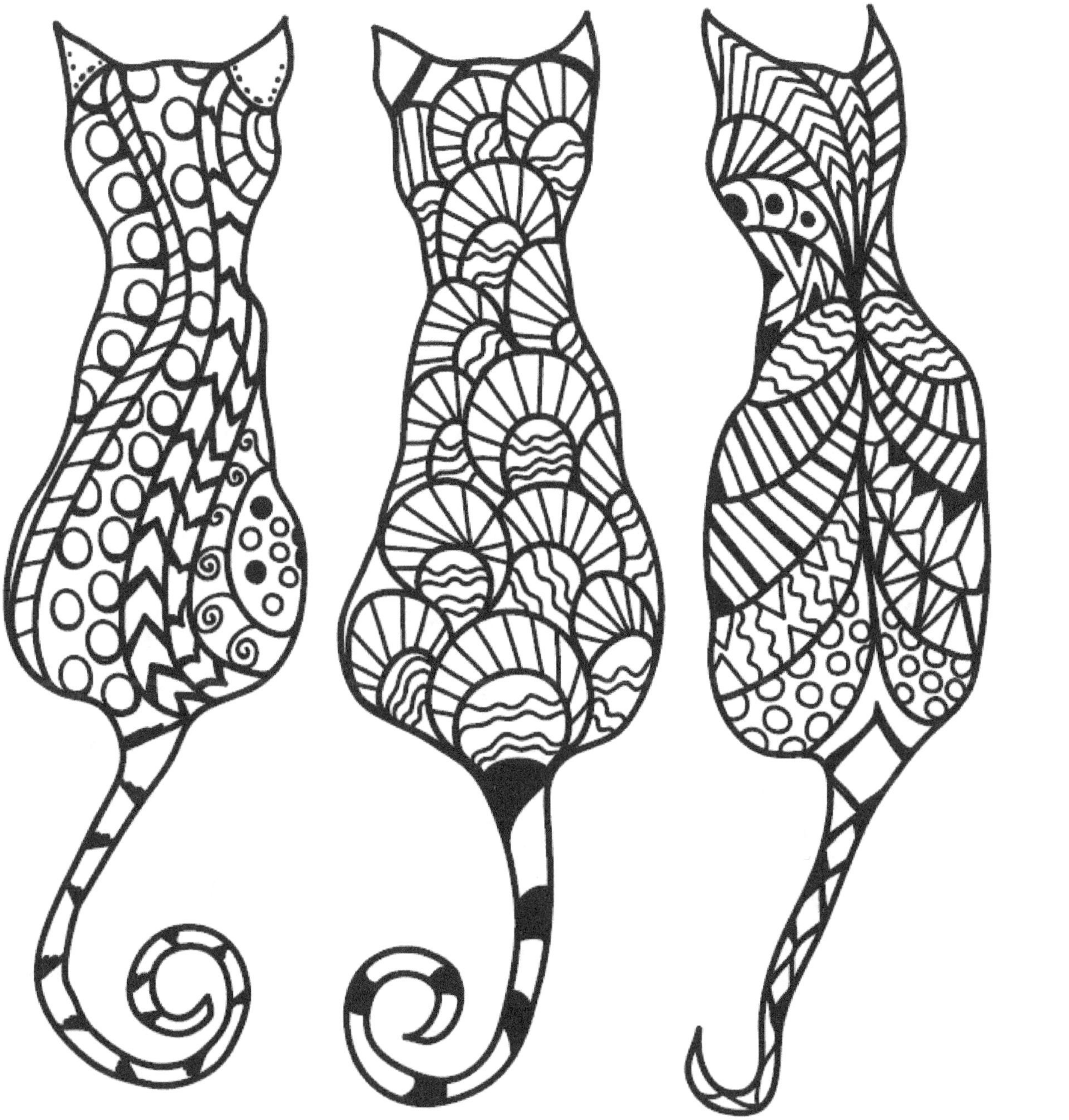

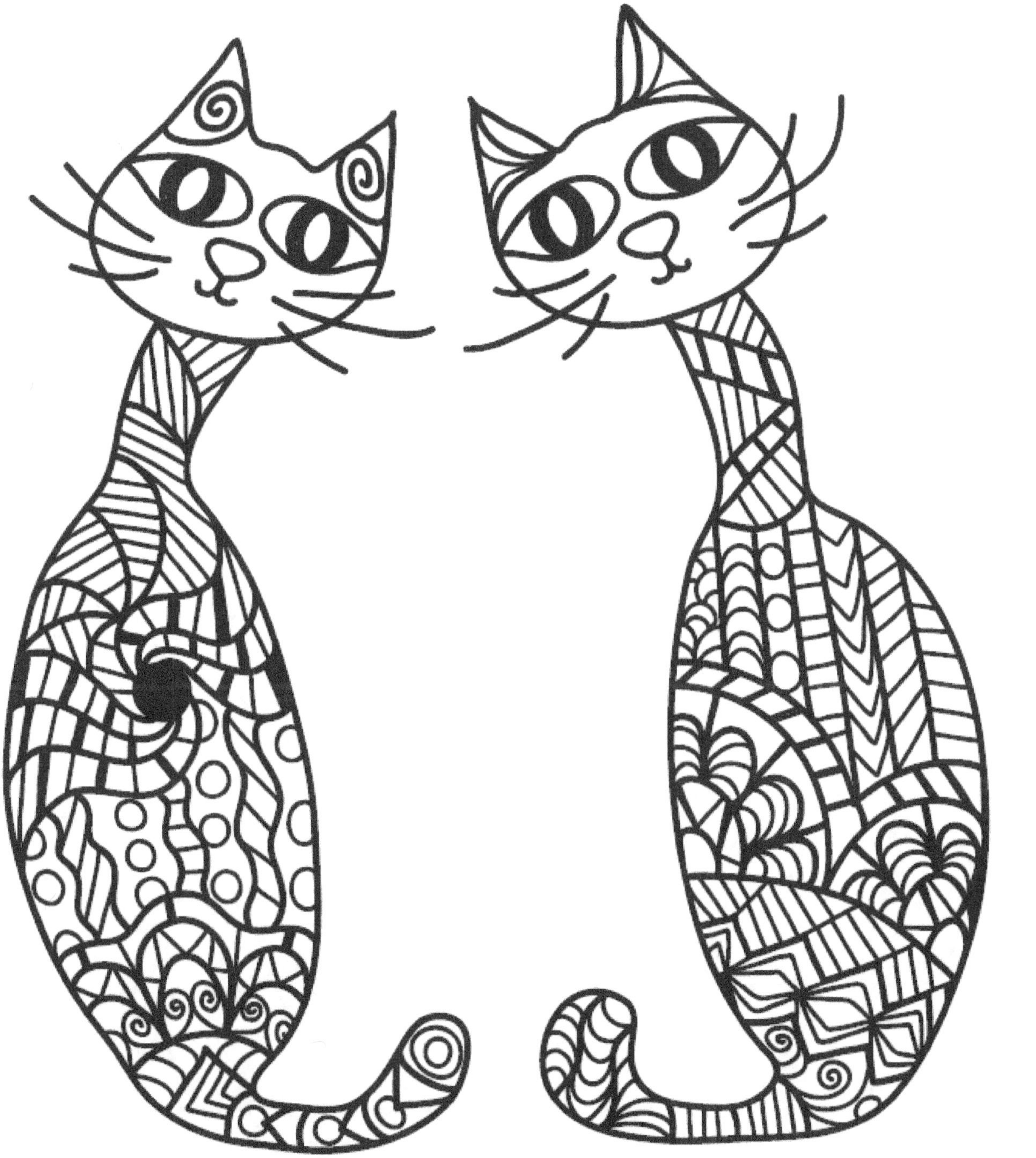

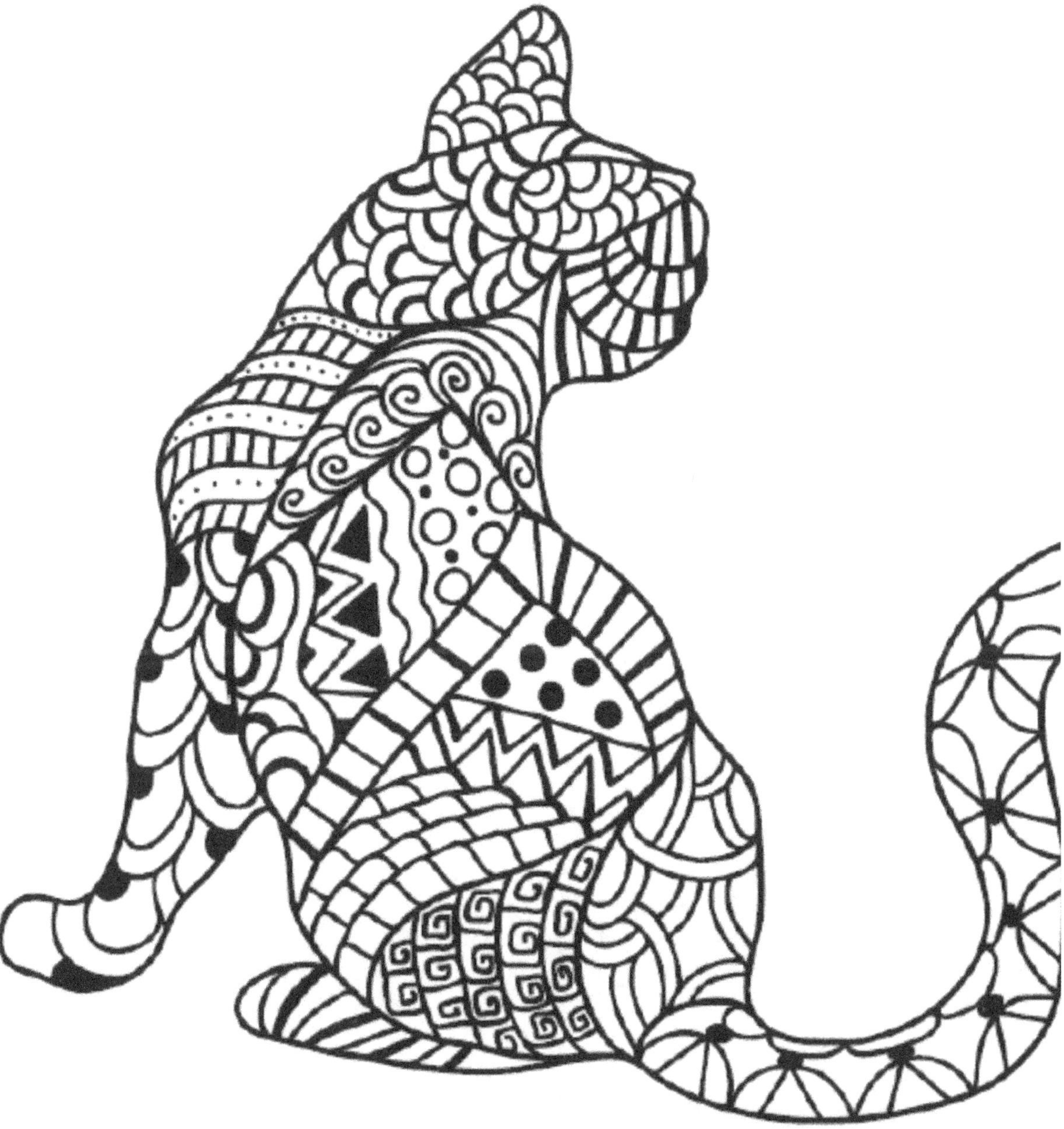

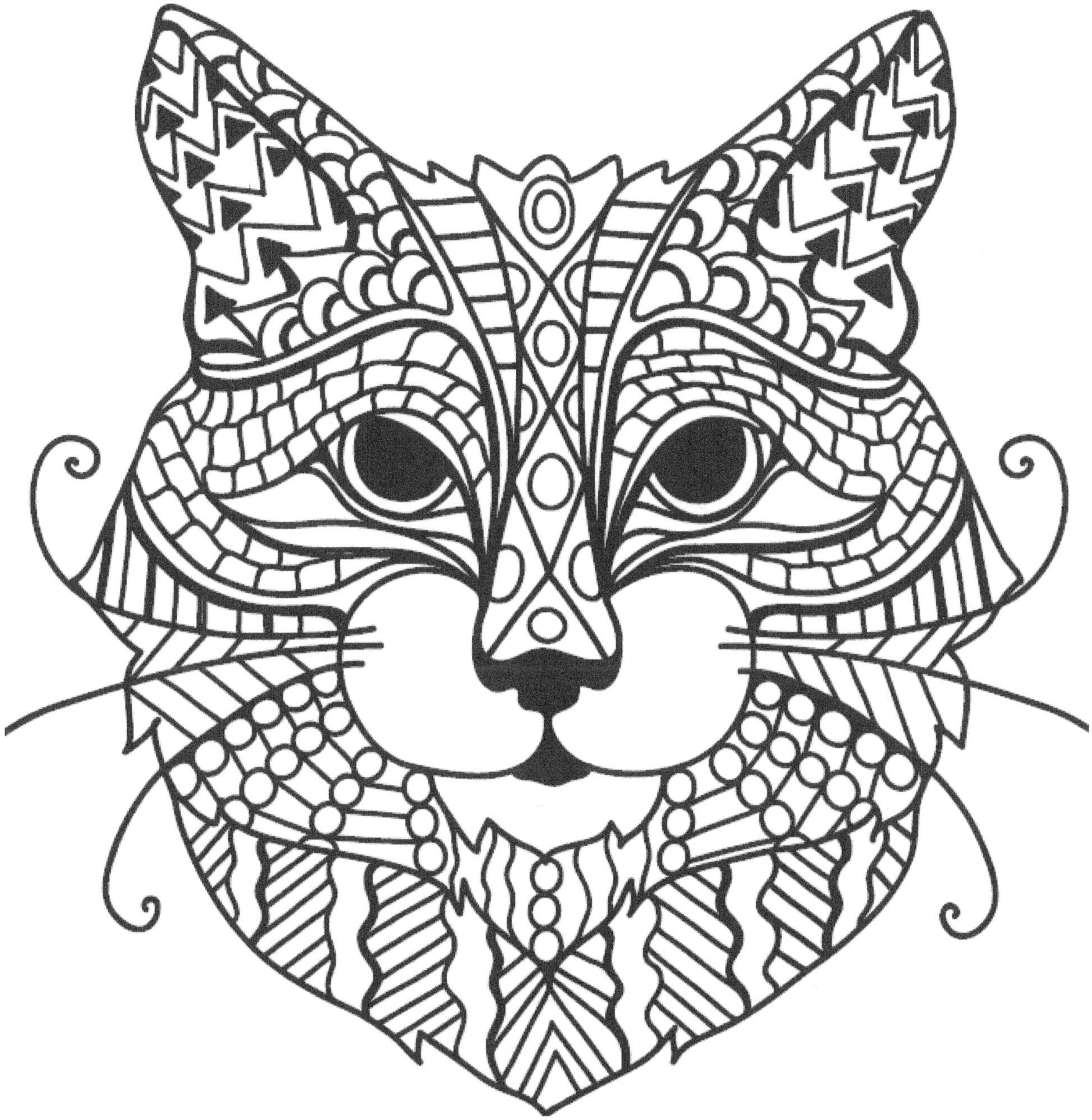

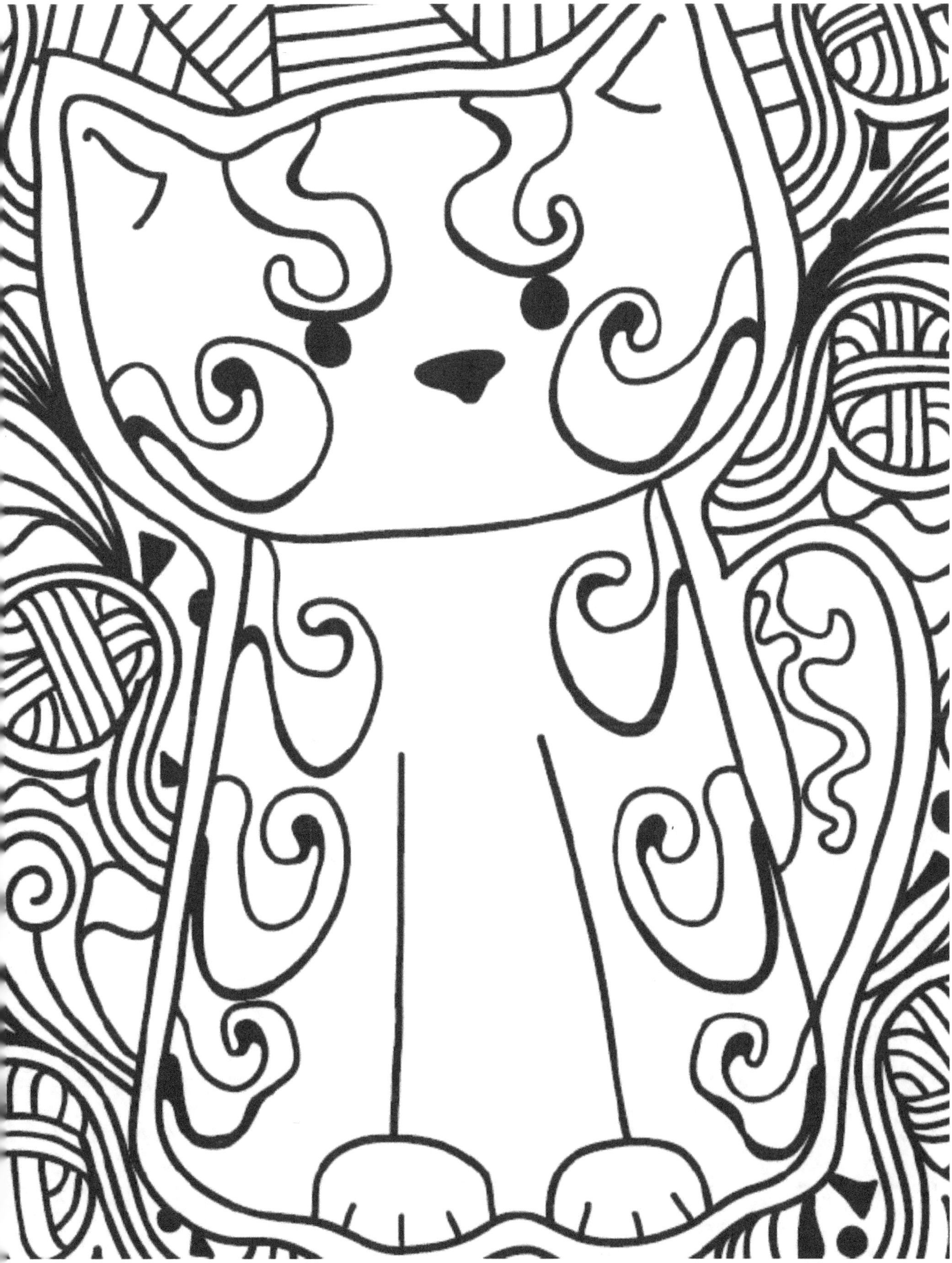

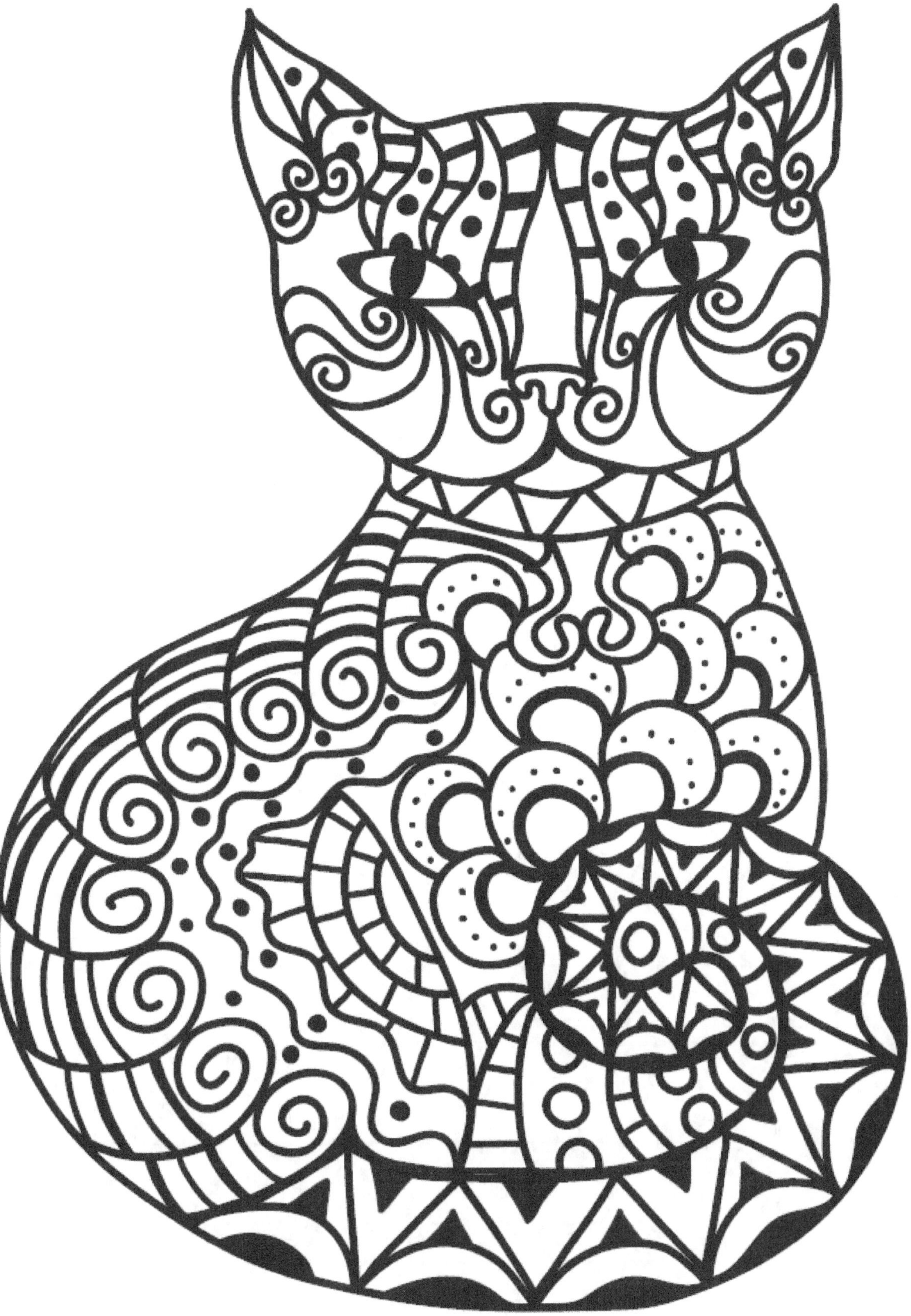

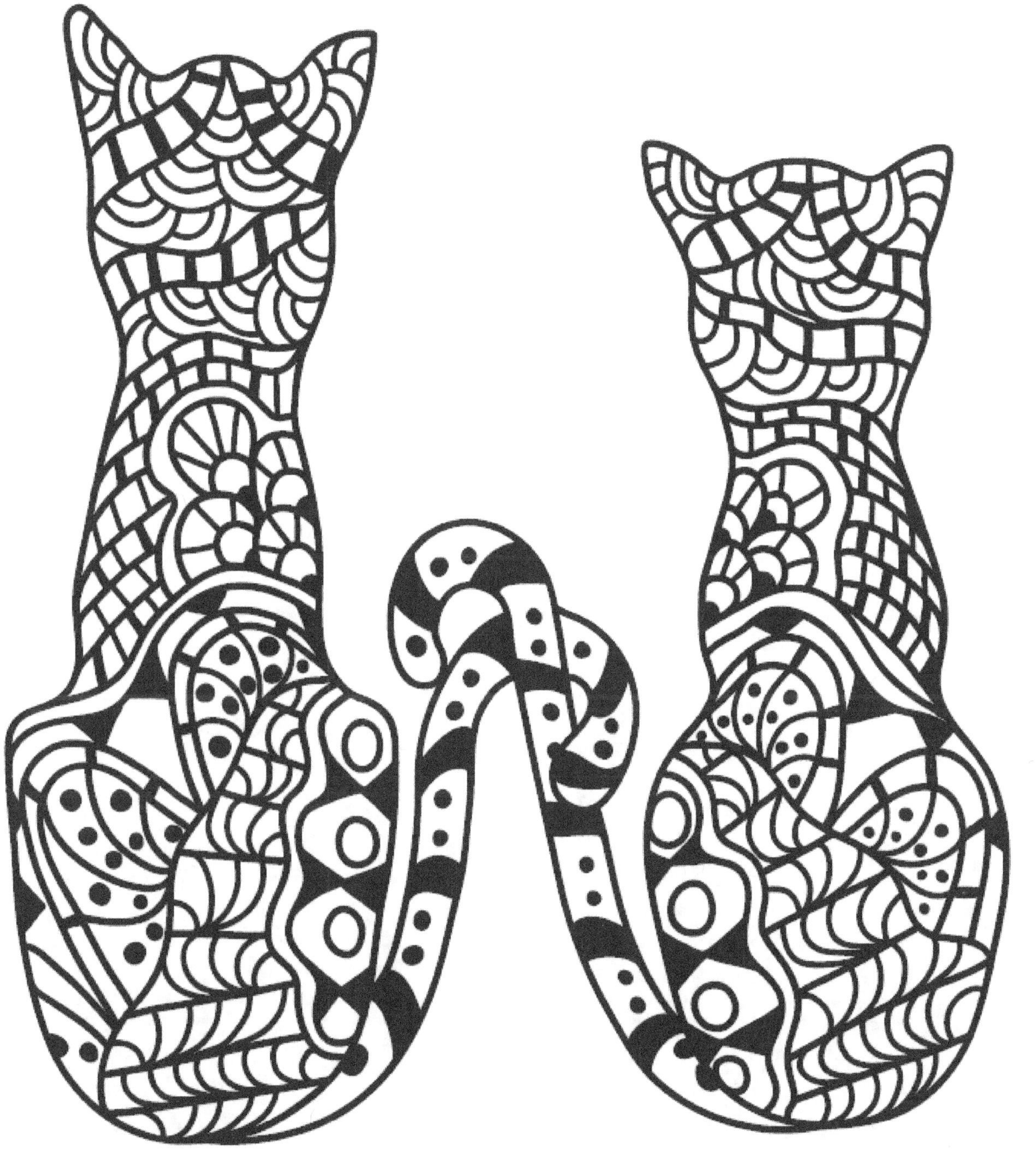

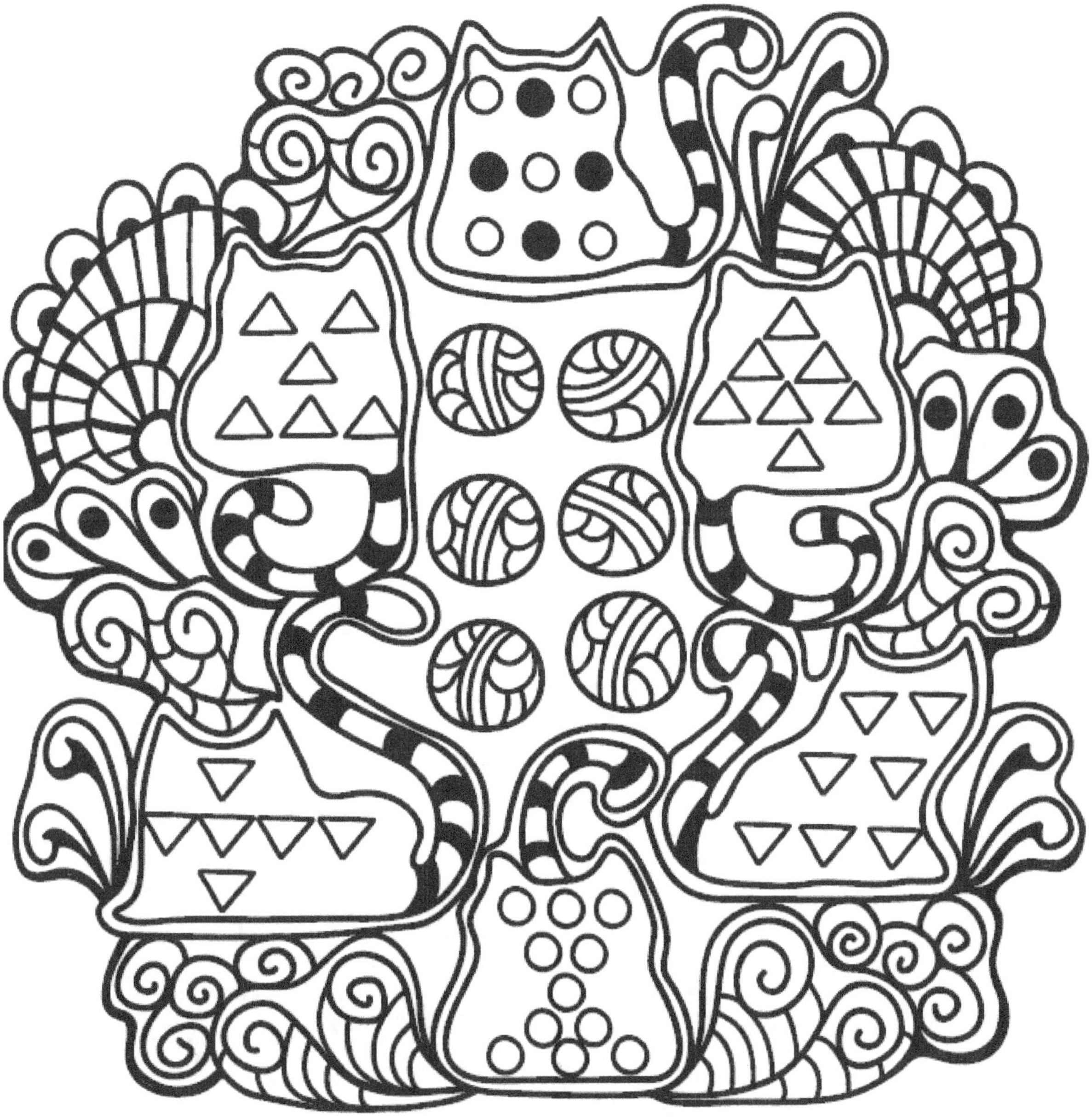

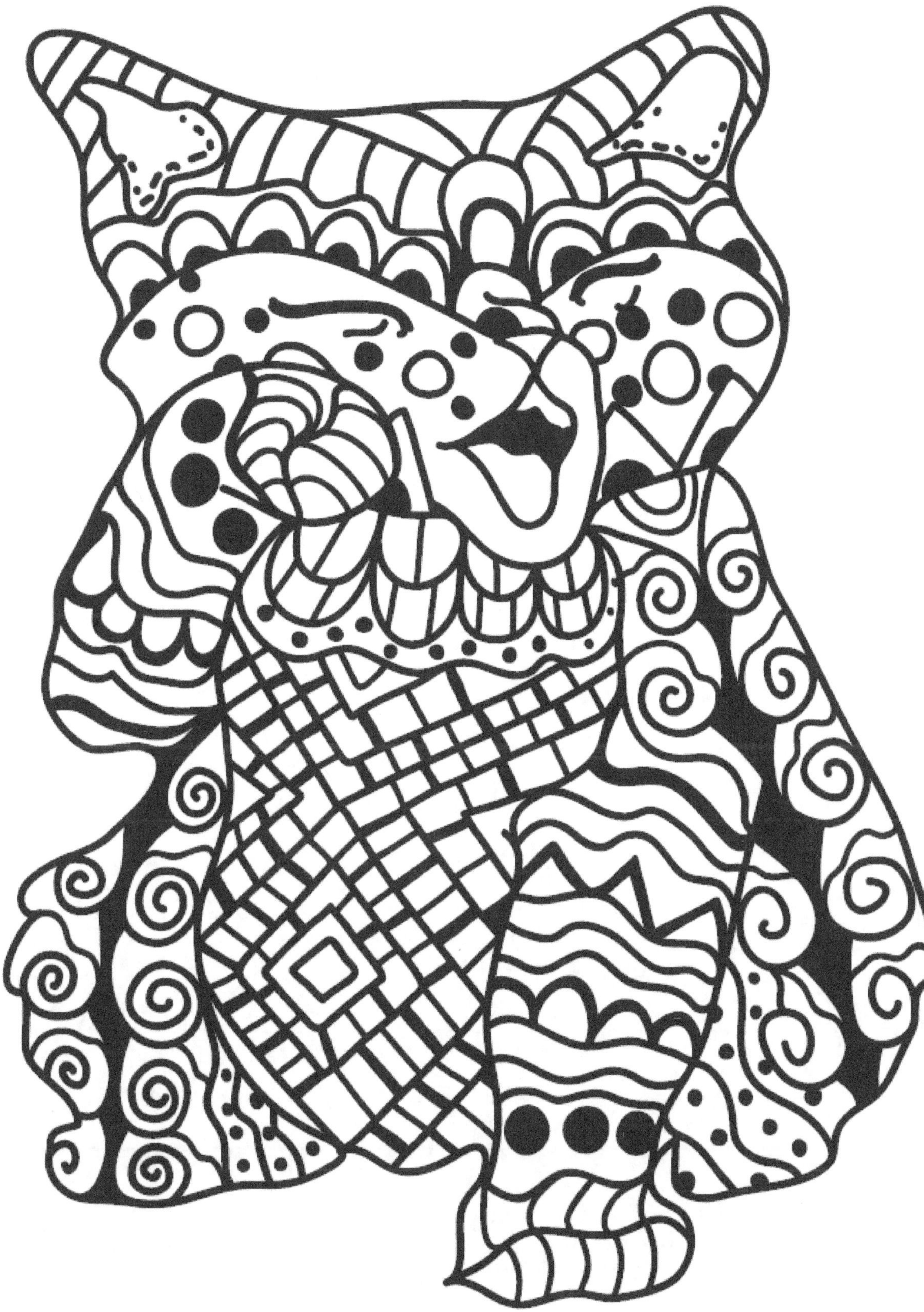

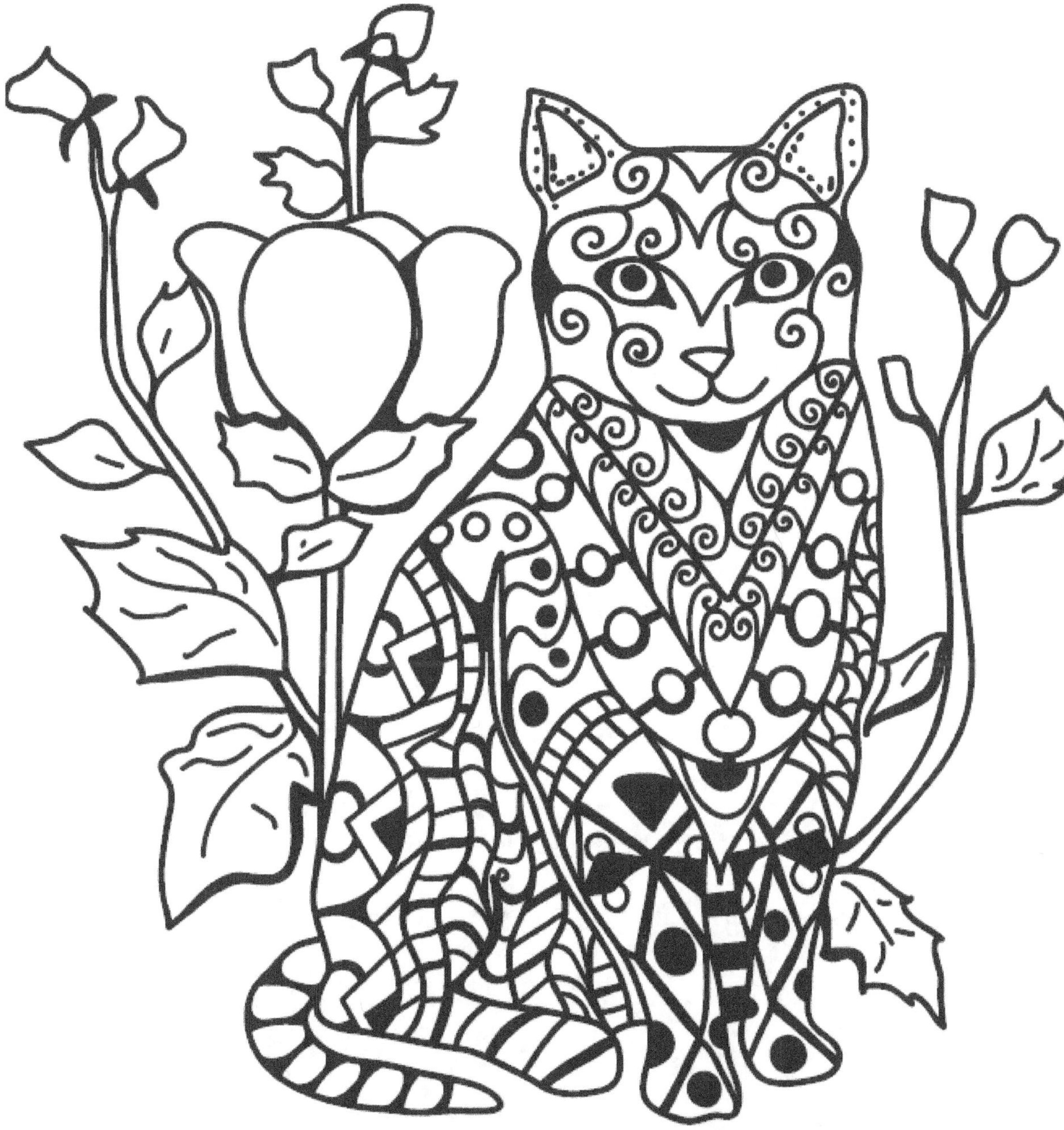

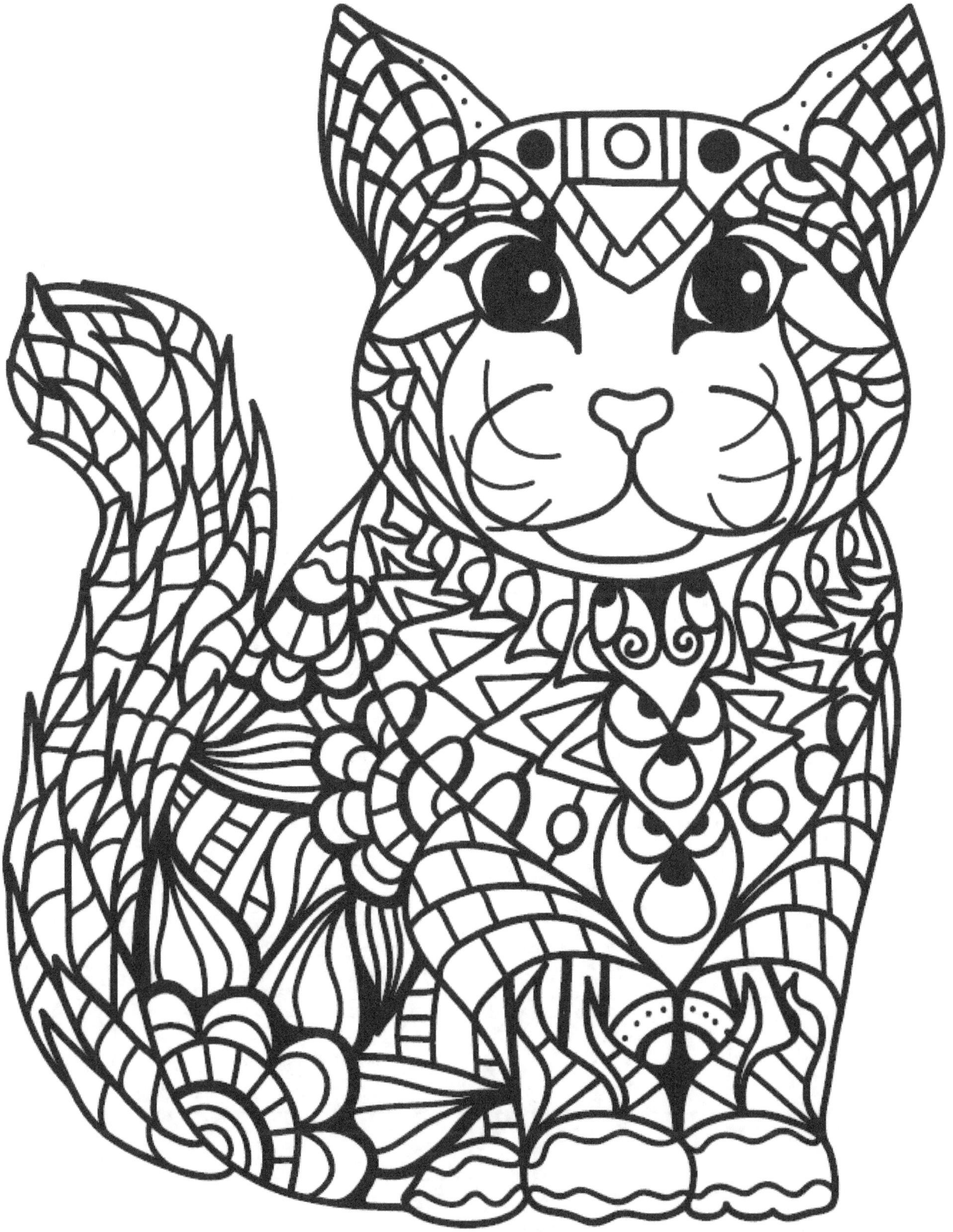

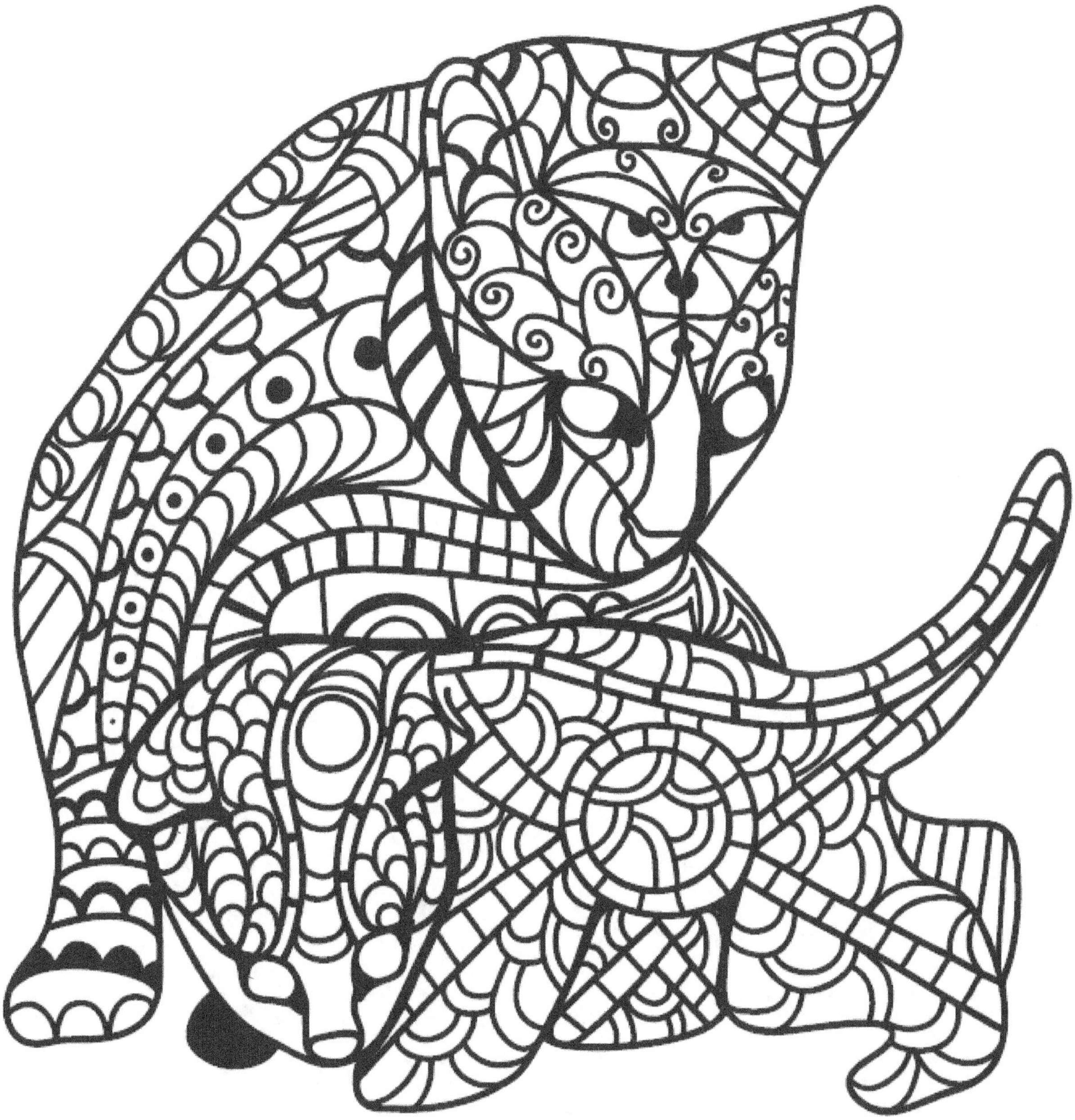

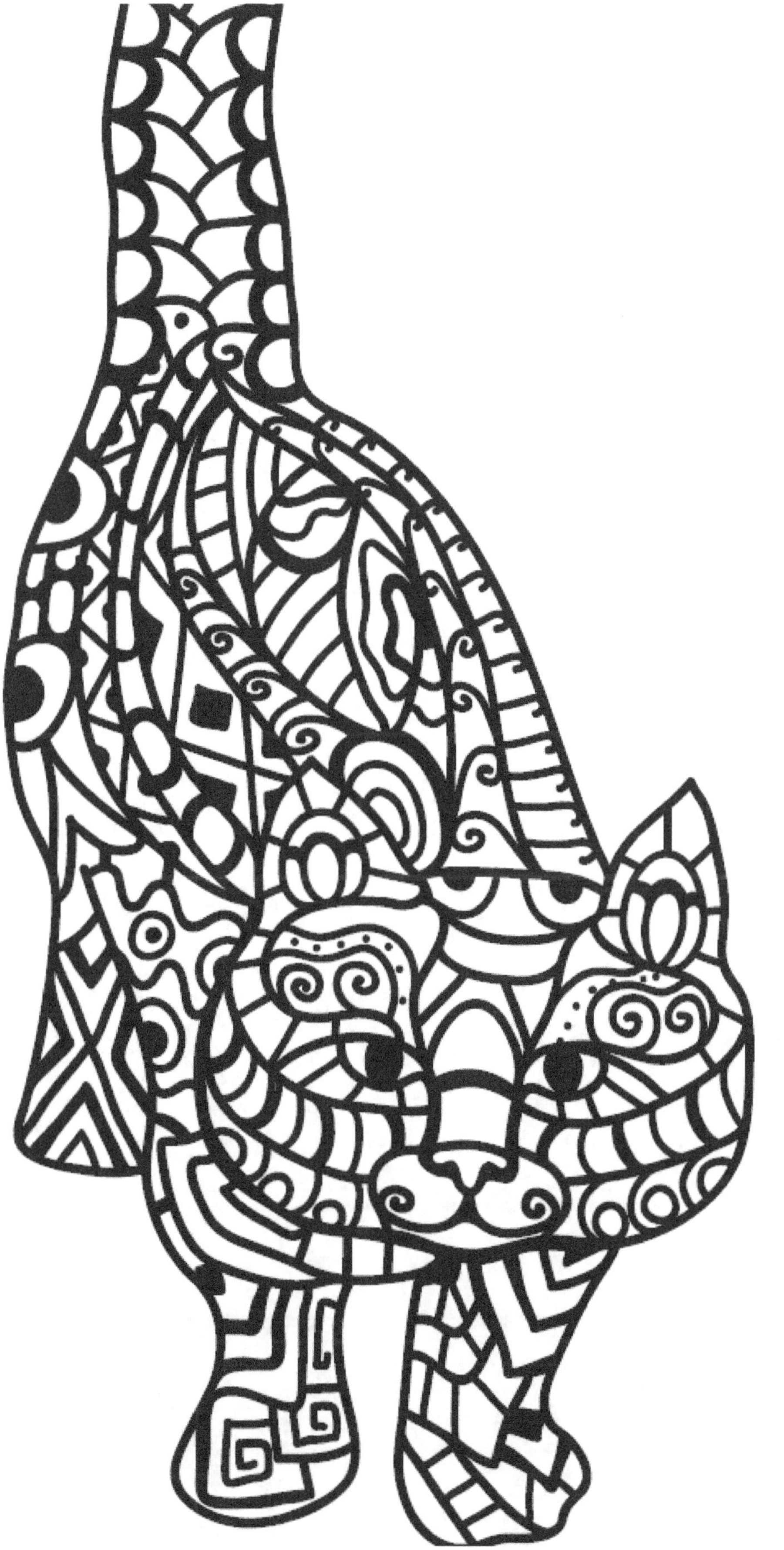

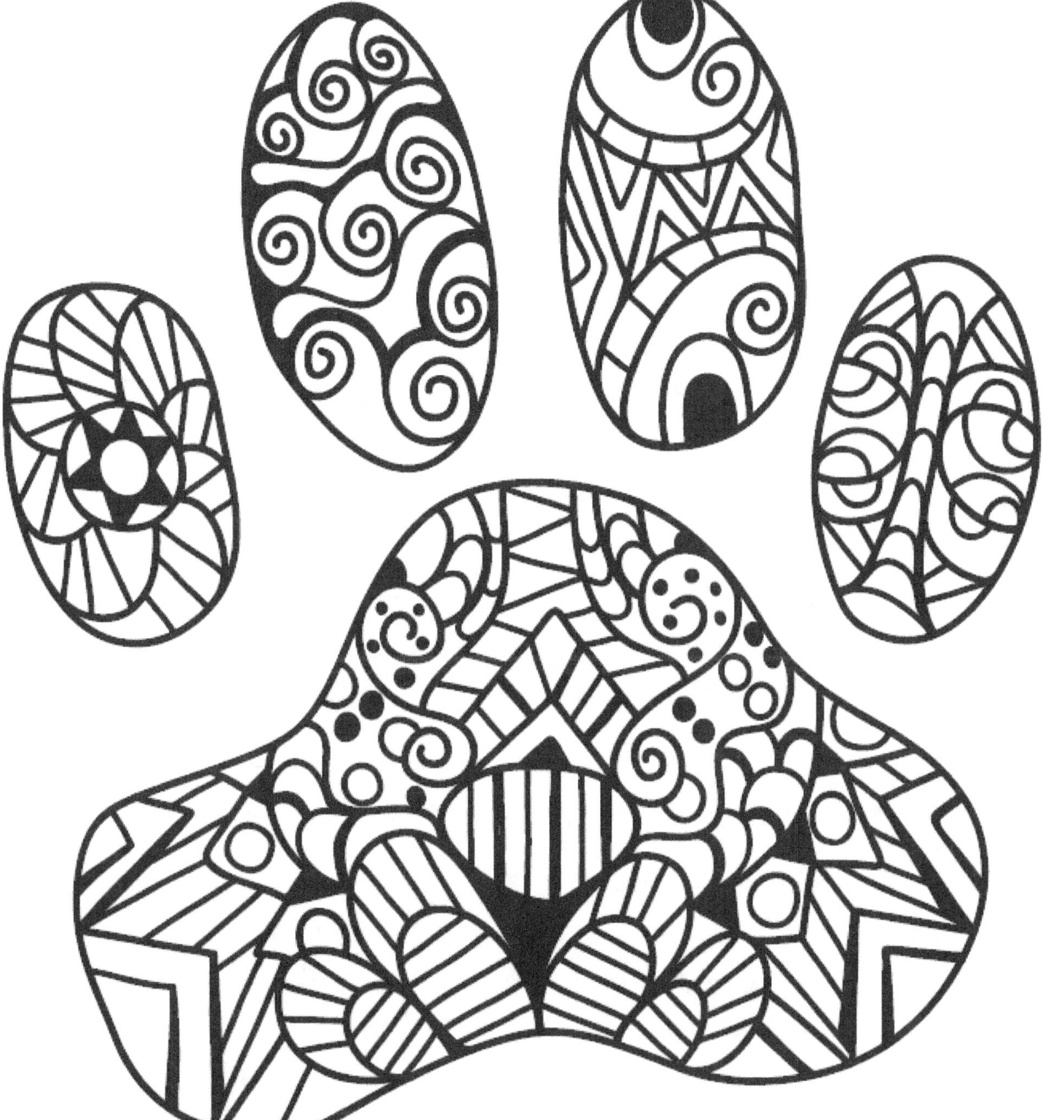

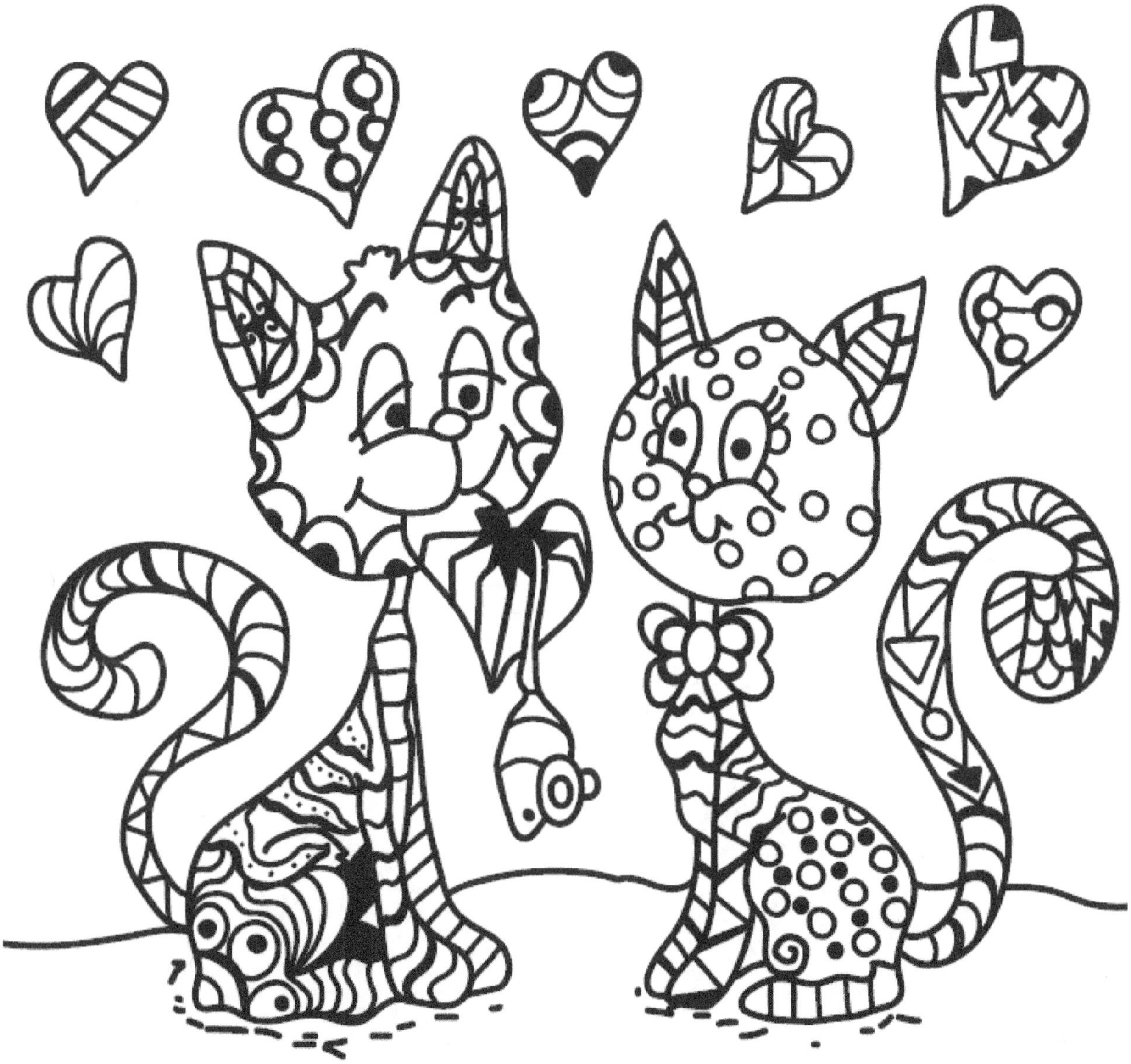

Cat Coloring Pages

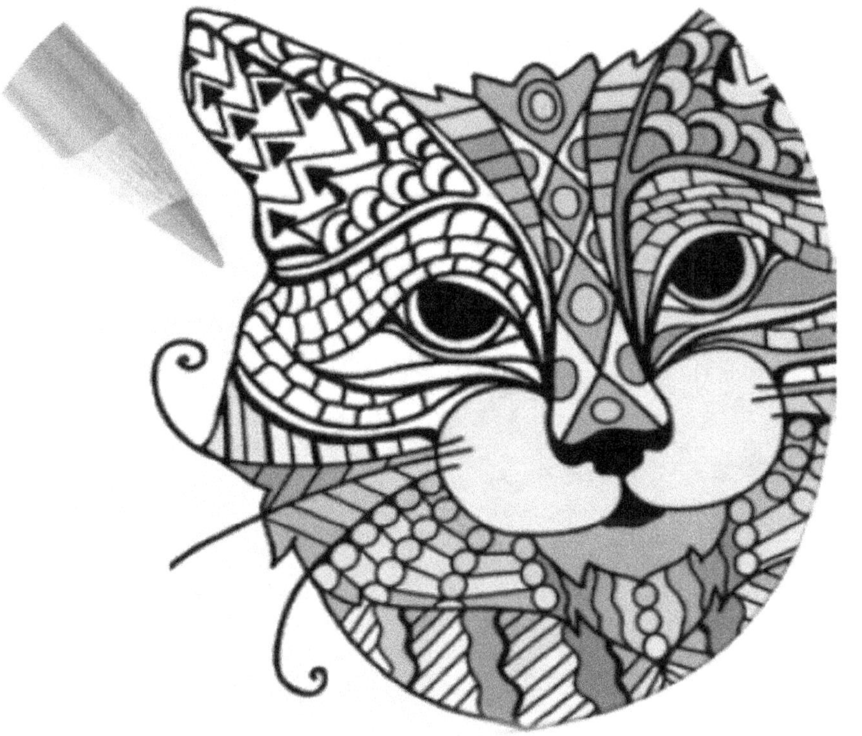

www.ingramcontent.com/pod-product-compliance
Lightning Source LLC
Chambersburg PA
CBHW080958220526
45467CB00008B/2610
9798689723747